Flowers for Special Occasions

FRESH WAYS WITH FLOWERS

Flowers for Special Occasions

SUSAN CONDER · SUE PHILLIPS · PAMELA WESTLAND

HAMLYN

Acknowledgements

Caroline Arber 38, 40(T), 56; John Bouchier 79, 80, 81, 82, 83;
Camera Press 39, 73(B), 75(T); Chris Crofton 21, 22, 23, 77, 87;
E.W.A. 8, 9, 34;
David Garcia 2, 6, 10, 11, 12, 13, 25, 26, 27, 29, 49, 52, 57, 61, 65;
Nelson Hargreaves 3, 37, 41, 58, 59, 74, 75(B), 84, 85, 95;
James Jackson 71(T); Duncan McNichol 40(B);
Roy McMahon 19, 30, 31, 33, 35, 50, 51, 53, 70, 88, 89;
Mondadori Press 18, 36, 71(B); Jane Pickering (Artwork) 44, 94;
Sandra Pond (Artwork) 14, 28, 64, 80, 86;
Pronuptia de Paris "Nadine" 55;
M. Smallcombe 15, 16, 17, 43, 44, 46, 47, 62, 63, 66, 67, 68, 69,
91, 92, 93; Syndication International 72, 73(T);
John Woodcock (Artwork) 13, 52.

The publishers are grateful for the help of the following:
Gail Armitage, Annabel Carter, Laura Lee, John and Bett Wareing.

Contents

Introduction

Flowers make wonderful decorations, and on special occasions it is particularly appropriate for them to form a focal point in the general setting. Indeed, without flowers, a special occasion would be far less memorable. Even a reluctant flower arranger can usually find that little extra time to compose a display to make all the difference to a special day.

Special occasions may occur at any time of the year, so both fresh and dried flowers are used in the arrangements in this book. There is no reason why a party in the bleak midwinter cannot be just as visually exciting and lavish as its summer counterpart. Of course, traditional holidays are not the only times when flowers will be appreciated. Any celebration, from a graduation to a welcome home party is an ideal time for you to show off your flower arranging talents. Floral decorations make a celebration extra special and particularly delightful for your guests.

Many of the arrangements in this book are illustrated with step by step photographs. These are particularly helpful for special occasion arrangements, which are often more elaborate than everyday displays. This can make the task less awe-inspiring and more fun for someone new to flower arranging, and certainly makes it easier to do.

Entertaining at home is the ideal time to give your creative talents full rein and to design floral displays to impress your guests. The original and exciting ideas in this book range from displays suitable for a formal dinner to the novel idea of a tea-time sponge cake flavoured with rose water.

Flowers and romance are an inseparable combination and what more romantic time of year is there than St Valentine's Day? A floral gift on 14 February will always be appreciated, and both fresh and dried flower displays will make it a Valentine's Day to treasure.

Weddings are occasions that really do demand flowers. The perfect flower arrangements for this most special occasion include pew-end designs for the church and children's decorations.

Seasonal celebrations, such as Christmas and Easter, are times when flowers look especially lovely in the home. Ideas and suggestions for both traditional and innovative ways to use flowers are sure to spark your imagination and make the festive holidays better than ever.

Don't forget that children, too, appreciate flowers. When you are planning a birthday party, you could try the novel arrangement with bright crayons or an idea of your own to liven up the day.

Flowers are always beautiful or striking and by using this book you can compose displays which will transform an important event into a true celebration. When your guests leave, they will take with them a vivid floral picture and even a sweetly fragrant memory.

Entertaining Ideas

IMPRESS YOUR GUESTS WHEN YOU ENTERTAIN WITH FLORAL ARRANGEMENTS THAT HAVE STYLE.

Flickering candles provide the perfect atmosphere for a romantic arrangement of white flowers. The polished silver candlesticks and glass table top reflect the light and add to the beauty of the arrangement. (BELOW)

There is nothing more delightful than welcoming your guests with flowers; and if it's a special occasion, you have the excuse to be extravagant. In a room full of people a subdued arrangement will get lost but a huge pedestal arrangement of roses and ferns will delight them and put them into the right mood for a party.

THEME PARTIES

If your party has a theme, use it in your choice of flowers. Select red roses for a ruby wedding, or, if you wish to create a traditional display, choose blue anemones, freesias, cornflower and larkspur for the christening of a baby boy. Throw a white party in a white room – ask all your guests to wear white, serve white wine and white food and fill the room with white or cream flowers: pale roses, snowy gypsophila, cool carnations, sweet stephanotis and chrysanthemum 'Esther Read'.

FORMAL OCCASIONS

Flowers add the finishing touch to a grand dinner party where you want everything to be perfect. In a large, old house or formal hotel function room with classic white, cream and gilt decor, choose a tall and densely massed arrangement in an urn positioned on a sideboard, preferably reflected in a large ornate mirror. Choosing only white and cream flowers and teaming them with variegated foliage creates a look of unrestrained elegance, a dignified complement to both the room and occasion. For such a display select agapanthus, tuberoses, lilies, bouvardia, stephanotis and gerberas.

Use the same flowers in a twin display on the mantelpiece and for pedestal arrangements that could flank the door to the room where the party will be held. Although the colours of white and green may be discreet, you can be sure that the grandeur of these bouquet arrangements

A mantlepiece display of roses, lilies and mimosa is perfect for a formal dinner party. Sprays of roses and aster 'Monte Casino' on the table do not restrict the guests' view. (LEFT)

will not be lost on your guests. Such displays can impress because of their sheer size, and because of the contrast they provide with the strict lines of symmetry of a classical interior. Table arrangements of variegated laurel and white roses ornamented with white candles would complete the magnificent picture.

MODERN SURROUNDINGS
In an ultra-modern setting, such traditional arrangements would look fussy and out of place. If your room has stark geometric furniture, flowers are still able to complement your decor if you plan an arrangement which is extremely simple and striking. For a formal occasion, you can choose one type of the most exotic and luxurious flower that you can find. These might include white canna lilies, orchids, anthuriums or strelitza.

In such a setting, just a few fascinating flowers in a clear glass flask needing no

mechanics will impress your guests more than an intricate arrangement. Dramatic flowers look particularly good teamed with a white dinner service.

THOUGHTFUL EXTRAS
When entertaining don't neglect the small token that shows your guests that you really care. When they go to the cloakroom they can be greeted by more subdued arrangements of flowers. Place a small arrangement on a table or on the windowsill of scented tuberoses and freesias framed in a lace doily in a bowl.

If you have friends and relations staying overnight, small bunches of flowers in their bedrooms will be appreciated. Try to avoid elaborate arrangements, hectic colours and heavy scents. Confine flowers to the dressing table – hands reaching out in the middle of the night for water may knock over a bedside table display. Little baskets of flowers in shades of cream and white would be ideal.

STEP *by* STEP

Candles and Tumblers

T his elegant dinner party display combines flowers, foliage and candles in a cluster of chunky blue glass tumblers. The glasses can be arranged in various attractive patterns, depending on the shape of the table and according to your taste. (FAR RIGHT)

D ifferent effects can be achieved by placing the miniature vases of flowers on the table either tightly bunched or in a linear fashion as here. (BELOW)

Flickering candles and a cluster of deep-blue tumblers filled with different flowers make an enchanting display, ideal for an informal dinner party. The warm glow of light adds a romantic touch.

This floral display is foolproof, takes only minutes to arrange and is bound to be a conversation piece. When arranging flowers, it's always satisfying to produce an effect that is both interesting and different.

Most flowers are suitable, so the choice depends on your taste, budget and colour scheme. Even huge flower spikes, such as gladioli or delphinium, which initially seem too big, can be separated and the

individual florets used. The green, flower-like bracts of fresh bells of Ireland (*Molucella laevis*) used here, have been cut into sections with the bracts forming a ruffle around the base of a group of candles.

MIXING SIZES AND SHAPES

Try to have a mixture of delicate, medium-sized and large flowers, with some foliage for contrast. Ideally, the medium-sized flowers should be suitable for tight clusters – like the small rose-buds and spray chrysanthemums here. The large flowers should be sculptural – trumpets and outsized daisies such as the lilies and gerberas pictured here.

Any colour scheme can be adapted to this display, but it is sensible to choose one relating to your china and table linen or whole room scheme. Here, irises and blue-dyed gypsophila repeat the blue of the glasses and the plaid tablecloth.

For total elegance, alternate large orchids, such as cattleyas, with medium-sized orchids, like cymbidiums, and small spray orchids, such as Singapore orchids. For an informal summer lunch, alternate wild flowers – buttercups, cow parsley and wild daisies – for a pretty country feel.

Foliage plays a minor role in this display, but still needs careful selection. Some flowers, such as the irises and lilies shown here, come complete with foliage. Bear grass is featured in one of the miniatures.

A member of the lily family, its narrow graceful leaves can be up to 1m (3ft) long. Bear grass is sold in single bunches or in mixed foliage bouquets with ferns. The quantity of foliage needed is only small, so you may be able to find what you are after in your own or a friend's garden, or take a leaf from a house plant, such as a spider plant.

CHOOSING CONTAINERS

Seven blue glass tumblers are used here, but choose more or less as the setting requires. Odd numbers tend to be more interesting than even numbers. Clear or pale-tinted glasses could be used, but the flower stems would be visible, and would need careful arranging. Stemmed glasses are a more formal alternative; ornately cut crystal would help conceal the stems.

You could feature different but related containers – perhaps a collection of attractive hand-painted porcelain cups – each holding identical flowers.

FEATURING CANDLES

Candles always add a romantic touch, and can add height to a dinner table arrangement without creating a barrier between guests. White candles are very elegant, but you could choose pale or brightly-coloured candles to tone with the flowers. Try an interesting range of sizes. Used here are a short, stubby, candle, five tall, thin candles and two medium-sized candles.

CHOOSING THE SETTING

A long dining table is perfect for this display of glasses set out in a row, or place them in a circle in the middle of a round table, or in a square pattern on a square table. Lined up, the glasses look lovely on a mantelpiece or windowsill.

CREATING A MULTI-VASE DINNER PARTY DISPLAY

YOU WILL NEED

 1 *7 blue glass tumblers*
 2 *5 long, thin candles*
 3 *2 medium candles*
 4 *1 short, fat candle*
 5 *3 irises*
 6 *8 roses*
 7 *small spray of bear grass*
 8 *2 gerberas*
 9 *small spray of blue-dyed gypsophila*
 10 *2 spikes of bells of Ireland*
 11 *4 sprays of chrysanthemums*
 12 *1 lily stem floristry scissors*

1

2

3

4

1 Cut two medium-size candles to different lengths. Fix them in a glass with melted wax and fill each glass with water. Cut three irises to leave 5cm (2in) stems and add to the candles. Cut and curl the iris foliage round your finger and rest the leaves on the rim of the glass. Arrange the other leaves vertically.

2 Cut two gerbera stems to 5cm (2in) and rest the flowerheads on the rim of a water-filled glass. (Any left-over gerberas with bent or damaged stems can be used in this glass.) Don't worry if they overlap, but try to get them facing upwards like flat discs, in contrast to the round and spiky iris flowers in the display.

3 Surround the short, stubby candle with short sprigs of blue-dyed gypsophila. Ensure the gypsophila is positioned well away from the burning wick. Cut a lily stem down to 5cm (2in), and position the blooms together with some of their foliage in another glass. Add a strand of arching bear grass.

4 Cut five tall, thin candles to different lengths and fix into a glass. Make a ruffled collar around their base with cut sections of bells of Ireland. Fill two more glasses with water. Pack one with eight short rose stems; place the central rose a little higher than the others. Pack the other with four short sprays of chrysanthemums – arranging them to spill over the rim.

FIXING CANDLES IN AN IRIS VASE

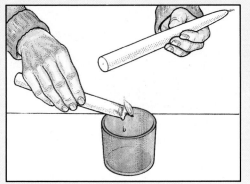

To fix a candle in a glass, simply melt some wax into the bottom, and press the candle firmly down. You can splay the candles out slightly, or have them vertical. Adjust as necessary, while the waxy base is still pliable. Cut the candles to different lengths but don't place them too close together in one glass as they will melt each other. Try floating candles or long-lasting nightlights as interesting alternatives.

STEP *by* STEP

Fruit and Flower Arrangement

Fruit and flowers are a traditional decorative display combination, as beautiful today as they were a hundred years ago, when the Victorians made fruit and flower displays on tiered ornamental stands, or epergnes. Here is a modern interpretation of the theme that makes a tempting table centrepiece for a party.

The display is all-round and informal, built on two florist's foam blocks, taped to a flat, round serving tray. Four small wicker baskets are wired around the edge of the blocks. A generous, round mass of fresh flowers and foliage is built up around the baskets, concealing the foundation and, finally, the baskets are filled with fruit.

You can make the basic display on the morning of the party, or even the night before, if you've got somewhere cool to keep it, but wait until the last minute to add the fruit.

CHOOSING THE FLOWERS
A cool green, yellow and white scheme is appropriate for late summer evenings, but you could substitute pink or blue for the yellow, or eliminate the third colour, and stick to white and green.

White bridal gladioli have a delicacy lacking in large-flowered forms. Spiky flowers with a similar form include montbretia, schizostylis and ixia (African corn lily). For a cheaper alternative, use white spray carnations.

Short-stemmed, creamy white and yellow hybrid roses add a touch of romance. Pure white or pink roses could be used. Another alternative is to buy spray roses, with several small blossoms per stem; they're more expensive, but you need fewer stems. For a cheaper ingredient, use godetias or scented pinks, which come in white as well as pink.

ADDED FRAGRANCE
Yellow freesias add fragrance and beauty; white, cream or mauve freesias could be used or multi-coloured bunches. For a long-lasting alternative, use green-white chincherinchees.

Singapore orchids are amazingly cheap

WIRING FRESH FRUIT

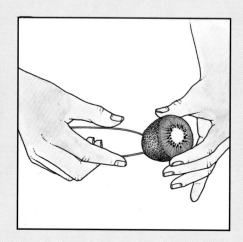

As well as displaying small fruits alongside the flowers in open baskets, make them an integral part of the arrangement. Wire fruits, such as gooseberries, lychees, strawberries, kumquats and grapes, on lengths of stub wire and insert the wire stems into the foam. The bright colours and varied textures of the fruit skins will contrast with the softer colours of the flowers. For a stunning effect, cut a kiwi fruit, in half to reveal the attractive inner flesh. Wire each half separately on lengths of stub wire. Push the wire through the base of the fruit and bend into a hairpin shape.

in Britain, considering their exotic origins and appearance. As well as the white featured here, they come in yellow, acid green, shades of purple and a new peach colour. Florists sell them in single-colour and mixed bunches.

White lilies add contrasting scale, but yellow or pink ones could be substituted. For additional fragrance, choose 'Ma-donna' or 'Stargazer' lilies; however, use them sparingly as they are quite expensive.

Moluccella, or bells of Ireland, seems an unlikely ingredient, since it's enormously tall compared to the other flowers. Here, it's cut into three pieces, and used to infill the arrangement.

Blue-dyed gypsophila is the most un-

This beautiful table arrangement of fresh seasonal fruit and flowers is sure to impress your guests. (ABOVE)

usual flower in the arrangement. White gypsophila or fennel flowers also would provide a lacy touch.

CHOOSING THE FOLIAGE

Bear grass, like the moluccella, is too long to be used its natural length in the design, so it is cut into thirds and inserted to make a pretty, linear fountain over the flowers. Slender stems of broom or ornamental grass, such as variegated sedge or pampas grass, could be substituted.

The sicklethorn fern (*Asparagus falcatus*) is so called because of its thorny stems. It's not often seen as florist's foliage, but makes a lovely, long-suffering houseplant, and can reach 1.8m (6ft) or more in height. You can use any other

asparagus fern instead, or fishbone cotoneaster stems.

Ivy from the garden, or from a house plant in need of pruning, is used as filler foliage, and to soften the outline of the display. Variegated ivy or the pretty yellow cultivar 'Buttercup' could be substituted.

Cineraria maritima, or dusty miller, is a member of the daisy, or Compositae, family and a popular bedding plant. To prevent wilting, put the stems in boiling water for a few seconds, then leave them in cold water for a long drink.

CHOOSING THE FRUIT

Grapes, passion fruit, cherries and raspberries are shown in the tempting nibble

MAKING A FRUIT AND FLOWER TABLE DISPLAY

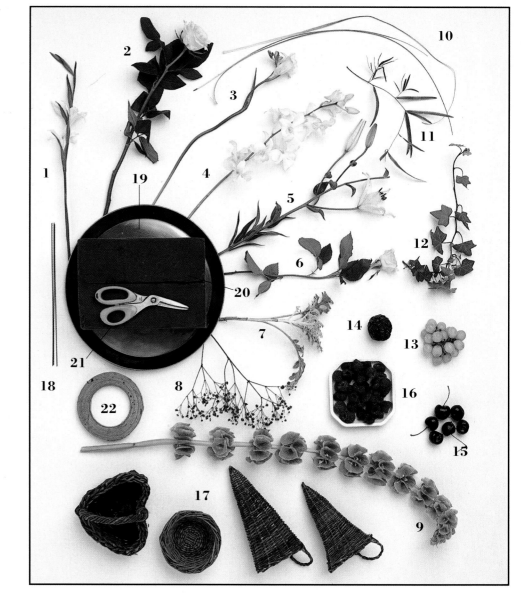

YOU WILL NEED

 1 *4 bunches of bridal gladioli*
 2 *1 bunch of white roses*
 3 *5 bunches of freesias*
 4 *3 stems of Singapore orchids*
 5 *1 bunch of white lilies*
 6 *1 yellow rose*
 7 *4 stems of Cineraria maritima*
 8 *¼ bunch of blue-dyed gypsophila*
 9 *1 stem of moluccella*
 10 *5 stems of bear grass*
 11 *3 stems of asparagus fern*
 12 *6 trails of ivy*
 13 *a small bunch of grapes*
 14 *4 passion fruit*
 15 *a handful of cherries*
 16 *a punnet of raspberries*
 17 *4 small assorted wicker baskets*
 18 *stub wires*
 19 *tray*
 20 *2 blocks of florist's foam*
 21 *scissors*
 22 *florist's adhesive tape*

1

2

3

4

5

6

1 Soak two blocks of florist's foam. Tape them, side by side to a small serving tray. Attach a heart-shaped basket to the foam at the front using two stub wires inserted into the foam through the base of the basket. Secure the two corncupia-style baskets at either side so that they face in opposite directions and one round basket to the back.

2 Snip trails of ivy from an ivy house plant and insert all over the foam. Frame the central basket with short stems of *Cineraria maritima* foliage. Cut a moluccella stem into three pieces and place behind the basket, one piece hanging over the display side.

3 Snip a stem of asparagus fern into small pieces. Dot it around the display. Cut the stems of bear grass into equal lengths. Insert them into the middle of the foam so that they spray out fountain-like, to add a contrast in height to lift the design. Spray the foliage to keep it fresh.

4 Cut four white roses and insert them vertically above the heart-shaped basket. Cut another four stems short and place three in a cluster to one side of the basket and one rose on the other side. Cut the bridal gladioli and frame the central basket with them.

5 Insert one yellow rose to the right-hand side of the basket. Cut the freesia stems and insert throughout the arrangement. The freesias' soft stems may need to be wired. Yellow freesias are the most fragrant.

6 Cut the stems of gypsophila and insert throughout the display. Cut the Singapore orchid spray in two. Place one half on either side of the display. Fill each basket with small fruits.

G listening fruit and flowers combine in this more informal display. The split-open pomegranate with its wealth of seeds adds an extra lushness to this display. (RIGHT)

baskets, but a wide range of exotic and seasonal fruits are available from large supermarkets, ethnic shops and street markets.

Other suitable fruity possibilities include gooseberries; red or white blackcurrants; kumquats; strawberries; halved kiwi fruits; loquats or Chinese gooseberries, with their papery calyces opened and swept back.

Grapes are available all year round; in cool green or rich, warm red. Cut them into small clusters, so that they are distributed evenly throughout the design and so that they are not all eaten at once. You could fill each basket with a different variety of grape, as a special touch you could perhaps add a few grape leaves and curly tendrils from an ornamental vine in the display.

In this design, passion fruit, with its pip-filled pulp, is intended to look decorative, rather than to be eaten on the spot — it is usually strained and used to make drinks, sweets, jellies, jams and sorbets.

Raspberries are delightful, but blackberries or any one of numerous hybrid berries are available — tayberries, dewberries, loganberries or sunberries — all can be used instead.

For a more integrated look in your display, you could wire up small, individual fruits in complementary or contrasting colours — see box — and insert them among the flowers.

CHOOSING THE BASKET NIBBLES

For an autumnal display or Christmas table, fill the basket with a selection of nuts, such as walnuts, hazel nuts, pistachios, Brazil or pecan nuts, in shades of beige and brown and change the colour scheme of the flowers accordingly — rich russet colour chrysanthemums would be ideal.

Alternative ideas to fill the baskets could be with a selection of appetizers, such as crisps, peanuts, Japanese rice crackers or for a more spicy taste, Bombay mix. For a truly luxurious touch, fill each basket with cooked and chilled giant Pacific prawns, garnished with lemon wedges. Alternatively, fill the baskets with wrapped mints, chocolates or sugared almonds, to accompany after dinner coffee and drinks.

CHOOSING THE CONTAINER

The arrangement shown features circular, heart-shaped and cornucopia wicker baskets but four identical baskets would work just as well. It's easy to wire wicker baskets in place, and, unlike plastic containers, they look as attractive empty as full. Hardware and Oriental shops usually have a good choice of suitably sized wicker baskets; some French cheeses are packaged in little wicker baskets, which are ideal for flower arranging.

PARTY TABLE SETTINGS

Roses frequently feature in flower arrangements and are always popular. Here are some party ideas.

Planning the flowers for a family birthday party or other special occasions can be just as much fun as organising and preparing the food.

If the party is an informal gathering for friends, set the scene for the food and a centrepiece arrangement by decorating the tablecloth with several varieties of foliage. Loop trailing ivy or smilax across the front and sides of the drape or scatter rose-buds across the table top. You could pin single flower and leaf sprays, such as a rose with a few leaves, over the cloth or fix flowerheads to the surface with loops of adhesive tape.

For a floral effect popular in north African countries, arrange the main dishes on a buffet table then scatter flowerheads or petals between them like confetti. Alternatively, position a simple bunch of flowers in the centre or at one end of the table.

Cool desserts of succulent fruit and ice-cream can also inspire floral party pieces, particularly for summer days. Sundae glasses filled with flowers, marbles and fruit make a treat that looks good enough to eat.

Fill a tall sundae glass with coloured marbles, to secure the flower stems and to represent the layers of fruit. Stand it on a glass platter, accompanied by a small, shallow glass bowl. Fill the bowl and glass with late summer garden or florist's roses in full bloom. Choose large-headed roses in pastel colours to resemble scoops of whipped or ice-cream.

Add coloured straws and slices of vivid fruit, such as kiwifruit to complete the design.

As an alternative idea, still on the ice-cream theme, you can make floral 'ice-cream cones' by rolling up biscuit-coloured card, lined with tin foil. Insert damp foam inside. Lay the cones flat on a tray, alternating heads and tails. Fill the cone tops with small flowerheads to resemble mouth-watering ice-creams.

For a sumptuous display, on a similar theme to the step by step dinner party display, combine fresh fruit and flowers in a lavish mound. Position a shallow dish on an old-fashioned cake stand. Place damp florist's foam in the dish and conceal it by surrounding the dish with ripe fruit. Insert mainly short-stemmed flowers and a few longer ones into the foam, to form a shape like a generous mound of ice-cream. Intersperse with a selection of glistening fruit impaled on cocktail sticks.

A mouthwatering display of roses and fresh fruits makes a novelty table setting. (BELOW)

STEP *by* STEP

Floral Ice bowl

Fantastic shapes in ice have always been popular at spectacular occasions. When the Princess of Wales toured Australia, a buffet held in her honour featured an ice swan.

However, ice bowls are not a modern idea, nor are they a Western invention. In 15th-century Turkey, when the nobles of the Ottoman Empire were renowned for their hospitality and excellent cuisine, Sultan Mehmet II made a surprise visit to the home of the Grand Mufti Abdullah Molla.

The Sultan was well pleased with the meal and remarked on the beauty of the serving bowls. However, he wondered why the fruit compote had been served in a different bowl from the rest of the dishes. The Mufti explained that he wanted the fruit chilled, but that chips of ice would have spoiled its texture. Instead, he had the fruit juice frozen in the shape of a bowl and served the compote in that.

The Mufti's fruit juice bowl can be duplicated in your own freezer. So can Princess Diana's ice swan – you can buy a rubber mould to make it in. The possibilities with ice are endless.

CREATING AN ICE BOWL
The principle of making a floral ice serving bowl is simple: you need two bowls that fit one inside the other with enough space in between them to fill with water for freezing into a fairly thick bowl. The more solid your ice bowl, the longer it will last. Freezer-proof glass bowls are the best to use as you can see the arrangement while you are making it.

As the bowl will be on the table for only part of the evening, the likelihood of it thawing is remote.

Yoghurt pots or margarine tubs would be suitable to use as moulds.

It is a good idea to make a trial ice bowl

beforehand to test your tap water. If the water is cloudy and yellowish, you won't achieve a crystal sparkle, however, you could use still mineral water instead. Alternatively, disguise murky water by adding a few drops of food colouring.

FLORAL DECORATIONS
Choose the flower decoration to suit your table setting and meal. The flowers and leaves must be unblemished as any flaws will be seen easily. Small, delicate flowers will keep the bowl frozen longer, or pick individual petals from larger flowers. Use edible flowers, unless you intend lining the bowl before filling it with your chosen food.

We chose a selection of meadow flowers and fresh herbs for our featured ice bucket, filled with ice cubes containing mint leaves and slivers of cucumber. Set on a silver tray surrounded by glasses and fruit, it makes a refreshing focal point for a drinks party. Alternatively, seal into the ice bowl sliced green olives, (black olives would seep juice), twists of lemon and orange, borage flowers and mint leaves. Freeze tiny flowers in the cubes for a complementary finishing touch.

FLAVOURS TO MATCH
Try including strawberry slices and flowers for serving strawberry ice-cream. If you are serving an indian meal, set an ice bowl with chillies, mint and star anise to hold a refreshing yogurt and cucumber dip. Add thin slices of cucumber and fronds of dill when serving prawn cocktail or fish mousse.

SEASONAL DECORATIONS
A delightful centre-piece for spring could be made with an ice bowl set with wild primroses and violets and filled with pretty eggs, lightly boiled quail's eggs for a first course, pale blue ducks' eggs for display,

A sparkling bowl of solid ice with a tracery of flowers and leaves set into its walls makes a magical feature for a summer dinner party. (FAR RIGHT)

or brightly decorated chicken's eggs for an Easter party.

Because flowers can be frozen so successfully, you could make a bowl when your favourite blooms are at their prime and use it in the depths of winter. Freeze snowdrops in spring for use the following Christmas, or freeze sweet pea blossoms for a birthday party later in the year.

FLOWER DISPLAYS ON ICE

If you want to use a floral ice bowl for a flower arrangement, remember not to add water or your bowl will melt. Choose flowers that last well out of water, such as roses and carnations. The ice will keep them fresh until after the party, when they can be plunged into water to revive them.

The bowl will last a surprisingly long time without melting and if you want to save it, just return it to its mould and top it up with water to use when you are next entertaining. If you are going to use the bowl as an ice bucket, make three batches of different brightly-coloured ice cubes to go inside it. This original multi-coloured display would be ideal for a children's party.

CREATING A FLORAL ICE SERVING BOWL

YOU WILL NEED

1 *a selection of edible flowerheads and herbs*
2 *1 cucumber*
3 *serving dish*
4 *2 tins or kitchen weights*
5 *1 ice cube tray*
6 *1 jug*
7 *freezer-proof glass bowls, 1 large and 1 small*
8 *1 kitchen plate*
9 *1 knitting needle or kitchen skewer*
10 *1 large bottle of still mineral water*

1

2

3

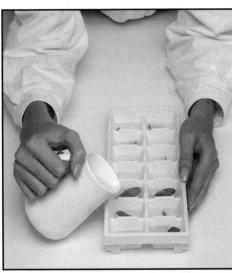

4

5

6

1 Half-fill the larger bowl with still mineral water and place the smaller bowl inside it. Weight the small bowl down with tins until the water level reaches almost to the rim of the outer bowl. The smaller bowl should not rest on the base of the larger one.

2 Wash the borage, daisies, marigolds, nasturtiums, buttercups, geraniums, mint and rosemary to remove insects and dust. Use a skewer to submerge them in the water between the bowls. Make an attractive pattern. Use plenty of flowers or they will float to the surface.

3 Gently place a plate on top of the bowls, making sure the smaller bowl remains in its central position. The plate will steady the weights and small bowl and prevent ice or debris dropping into the water. Carefully transfer the bowls to the freezer, making sure they stand level.

4 To make ice cubes, place mint and cucumber triangles into each ice cube tray. compartment. Half fill each with mineral water, so the leaves and cucumber float to the surface. Place in the freezer. When frozen, top up the cubes with water and return to the freezer until frozen.

5 To unmould, run cold water into the inside of the small bowl and release it. Run cold water over the outside of the large bowl and loosen it so the ice bowl is released. Smooth rough edges with a warm, damp cloth.

6 Stand the floral ice bowl on a silver tray or glass pedestal cake stand to show it off to best advantage. A tray with a slightly curved edge will prevent the ice bowl from sliding off the side. Empty the decorative ice cubes into the bowl.

STEP *by* STEP

Children's Party Flowers

Children, as much as adults, deserve attractive flower arrangements to mark the high spots in their lives – and birthday parties surely rank among the highest! Bright colours are always popular with children, and the anemones featured in this display provide a blaze of primary colours.

Set aside at least half an hour out of the time you've allowed for general preparations to tackle the flower arrangement. Once it's finished, keep it in a cool but draught-free spot until just before the party starts. That way, you'll get maximum 'life' and pleasure from the cut flowers.

A word of warning! Young children's enthusiasm can quickly overwhelm their 'party manners'. When the time comes for each guest to choose a coloured pencil prize, try to have them do it one at a time. You might even be able to make a game of it – putting numbered cards randomly under each place setting, for example, and having the children choose in numer-

ical order, or conducting a simple quiz, with the winner choosing a prize. Hold the base of the display while prizes are being selected, or stick it to a convenient spot on a low table with some blue tacky clay.

CHOOSING THE FLOWERS

Although there are traditional birthday flowers for each month – roses for June, carnations for January, and so on – this is too sophisticated an idea for most children, who simply want something bright and colourful to look at. If the birthday girl or boy has a favourite colour, however, you may want to base your display around that alone.

Some of the flowers used in this display are sold all year round; others, such as anemones, are seasonal, but can be easily replaced with equally beautiful seasonal flowers. All are relatively inexpensive and popular, and are widely available from florists, flower stalls and some high-street chain stores.

The florist's anemones (*Anemone coronaria* hybrids), often called 'de Caen' or 'St Bridget' anemones, provide the bright focal colour in this display. The goblet-shaped, black-centred flowers come in both single and double forms, and in mixed shades of purple, blue, red, pink and white – as well as in single-colour bunches. Here, a bunch of mixed colours and a bunch of deep violet-blue anemones are used – about 25 stems in all – with the violet-blue flowers providing the main colour theme.

When you get the anemones home, condition them by re-cutting the stems, dipping the ends in boiling water for a few seconds, then following with a long, cool drink of water, ideally overnight, before arranging them.

If you can't get anemones, china asters, with their flat flowers in shades of pink, white, mauve and blue, would be good

BUYING ANEMONES

Choose flowers that have just started to open. Avoid those with the petals opened out flat, as these are past their best. Anemones with extra-long stems are elegant but more expensive, and in this display, they would be wasted. If anemone stems are curving when you buy them, you can straighten them before arranging. Wrap them tightly in damp newspaper, with the flowers facing inwards, and leave in a bucket of cold water for a few hours, or overnight, in a cool dark spot.

substitutes, as would godetia, or satin flower, in its range of pinks and reds.

SWEET SCENTED FLOWERS

Freesias are included for their sweet scent as much as for their colour.

When choosing freesias, look for bunches with the lowest bud on each flower spike open or about to open. Lily of the valley, though more expensive, have an equally beautiful, lingering fragrance, and delicate charm. You could use them instead, perhaps combined with open 'Sweetheart' roses as the main flower.

Sprigs of gypsophila and spray carnations complete the floral palette. The spray carnations are creamy white, rimmed with red, to contrast with the more solid-coloured flowers, but white, pink, or scarlet spray carnations would be equally

A pretty floral display complete with crayons for prizes is perfect for a children's party. (LEFT)

effective. Gypsophila, the most popular 'filler' of all, is at its best in the pure white form, as used here. Choose sprigs with about two-thirds of the flowers open.

Variegated ivy and golden yew (*Taxus baccata* 'Aurea') are used to offset the warm floral colours. The yew is definitely a garden plant rather than a commercial one, but sprigs of cypress, though darker, could be used instead.

You can order variegated ivy from your florist, but will probably have to buy a bunch much larger than you need for this display. Plant some of the extra stems in an indoor pot. If fresh, they should root, and from the following year onwards, you'll have your own private supply. Don't just bury the cut end, though; cover the

entire length of the stem with 1.5cm (½in) of soil with the leaves above ground and keep well-watered in dry weather.

Asparagus fern (*Asparagus plumosus*) completes the trio of suitable foliage. This is a florist's standby – you should be able to buy it by the stem.

CHOOSING THE CONTAINER

In this display, the container is made up of large and medium-sized dessert or coupe pedestal glasses, one inside the other, and they are all but hidden by the flowers and foliage. Using a stemmed container is very effective, as it lifts the display off the table surface, allowing some material to trail and arch gracefully,

MAKING A CHILDREN'S PARTY DISPLAY

YOU WILL NEED

1 *25 anemones*
2 *bunch of freesias*
3 *small bunch of carnations*
4 *a few sprigs of gypsophila*
5 *2 stems asparagus fern*
6 *a few trails of ivy*
7 *a few sprigs of golden yew*
8 *large block of florist's foam*
9 *florist's adhesive clay*
10 *prong*
11 *2 cup-shaped pedestal glasses*
12 *coloured pencils*
13 *floristry scissors*
14 *knife*

1 Use the prepared containers. Cut 10 leaves, each with a short piece of stem attached, from the main trails of ivy. Insert the ivy leaves, evenly spaced apart, but overlapping, into the sides of the lower foam blocks, to form a horizontal 'collar', overhanging the rim.

2 Break off the leaf-like fronds from two stems of asparagus fern. Insert about half of them into the sides of the foam block, just above the ivy-leaf 'collar'. Using the remaining asparagus fern, make another horizontal 'collar' around the edge of the upper container.

3 Insert a small anemone with a 10cm (4in) long stem in the centre of the upper tier, to set the height. Shorten the remaining anemone stems to 5-7.5cm (2-3in). Insert a ring of large anemones above the ivy, then work up to build a dome.

4 Cut the golden yew into sprigs roughly 7.5cm (3in) long. Remove the lower needles from each sprig, and begin filling in the spaces between the anemones, to conceal the foam block. Prepare about 15 carnation flowers and buds with 7.5cm (3in) stems. Insert them randomly.

5 Cut the freesia stems to a similar length, leaving some a little shorter, others a little longer, for variety. Use them to add lighter areas of colour. The yellow freesias stand out especially, so keep them well apart. Add bunched sprigs of gypsophila.

6 When you are satisfied with the all-over density of the display, insert the coloured pencils, angled upwards towards the top, and out and downwards towards the bottom. Add one for each guest, but allow some extras.

and prevents the arrangement from looking heavy or dumpy.

Fixing up the two-tiered container couldn't be easier (see box). But you could, instead, use a two-tiered cake stand with moistened florist's foam block impaled on florist' prongs, round the central stem.

ALTERNATIVE PRIZES

Brightly-coloured pencils, toning in with the flowers, are featured here, but there are all sorts of alternative prizes you might like to try. Cellophane-wrapped barley sugar sticks, or, at Christmas-time, American-style red and white striped candy canes, would be ideal. Instead of inserting them directly into the florist's foam, wrap medium-gauge stub wire around them and insert the end of the wire into the foam. Lollipops can be inserted directly into the florist's foam block, but do this at the last minute, so the cardboard stick ends don't get soggy.

For very young children choose decorative pencils topped with heads of favourite cartoon or television characters. Older children are fascinated by curled transparent plastic drinking straws – these add just the right hint of 'trendiness' that an adolescent longs for. For an adult cocktail party, attractive or jokey swizzle sticks would be ideal. For the centrepiece of an Oriental dinner party, decorative chopsticks are the perfect, novel finishing touch.

CHOOSING A LOCATION

This flower arrangement is a genuinely moveable feast. Its first job is to grace the birthday party dining or buffet table, as shown, but it's far too attractive to dismantle once the party is over. Being an 'all-round' display, it is ideal for a coffee table or bedside table; the birthday boy or girl may want it in his or her room afterwards, as a reminder of their 'big' day.

As with any fresh flower display, it will last longer if you keep it away from heat, draughts, and direct sunlight. Because freesias and gypsophila are particularly vulnerable to ethylene gas damage, keep the display away from any bowls of ripe fruit and vegetables.

LOOKING AFTER YOUR DISPLAY

After the young guests have gone, you might want to adjust the flowers to close

PREPARING A TWO-TIERED CONTAINER

1 Stick four small balls of clay to the underside of the base of the smaller container, around the outer edge. Press the base of the smaller container firmly into the centre of the larger container, until it feels secure. Then, fix a pinholder to the bottom of the upper container with a ball of florist's clay.

2 Soak a large piece of florist's foam block until the bubbles stop rising, then cut off one end to fit the upper container, and press onto the pinholder, Cut three smaller pieces from the saturated foam block, and wedge them firmly into the bottom container, around the stem of the upper container.

W̶hen the birthday party's over, and the prizes are removed, the display takes on a new lease of life. Here, it is used as the sophisticated focal point in a modern living room, but it would be equally attractive in a less formal scheme, or as a pretty, scented feature on a bedside table. (LEFT)

any gaps caused by the removal of pencils or the actions of young hands generally.

Anemones are heavy drinkers, so keep the florist's foam block well saturated, adding more water daily, Anemones also have a habit of turning towards the light – charming in theory, but awkward in an all-round display, such as this one. If the light source comes from one direction – say, a nearby window – give the arrangement roughly a quarter-turn every day, to keep the flower stems relatively straight.

The asparagus fern will quickly drop its needles in a dry atmosphere, so an occasional spray-mist will keep it intact

for two weeks or more. If you've used Boston fern or *Asparagus sprengeri*, the same applies. Cut ivy will also last longer in a humid environment than in a dry one.

Anemones can be relied on to last at least four days, longer if well cared for. (Shortening their stems also helps prolong their life.) For freesias, a week is usually their outer limit. Longest lasting of all are the spray carnations, up to three weeks in cool conditions. Gypsophila, of course, dries as it ages, so you need never throw it away. Once the shorter-lived flowers die, re-use carnations and gypsophila with any remaining foliage to make a tiny display.

STEP *by* STEP

Tea-time Treat

Flavouring and decorating cakes with rose petals is a novel way of using edible flowers in cookery. The resulting cake is attractive and unusual enough to make tea time into a special occasion.

The light texture of a whisked sponge cake complements the delicate flavour of roses particularly well, but you could flavour and decorate cakes such as Victoria sponges that are made by creaming the egg and sugar mixture if you prefer.

MAKING THE CAKE

First make the whisked sponge cake. The ingredients used for the cake featured in the step by step are: three eggs, 75g (3oz/6 tablespoons) caster sugar, 75g (3oz/9 tablespoons) plain flour, a pinch of salt, 40g (1½oz/2½ tablespoons) melted unsalted butter and 1½-2 tablespoons of rose water. You also will need two 17.5cm (7in) sandwich tins.

Whisk the eggs and sugar together in a large bowl placed over a saucepan of hot, not boiling, water until the beater leaves a trail across the surface. Ensure that the bottom of the bowl is above the level of the hot water. Remove the bowl from the heat and continue to whisk until the mixture has cooled. Sift the flour and salt over the surface of the mixture and gently fold them in using a large metal spoon. Add the melted, but not hot, butter in a slow, steady stream and fold into the mixture. Lastly, fold in the rose water. Divide the cake mixture between two 17.5cm non-stick or greased tins that have been covered lightly in flour, smoothing the surface so that it is even. Bake in an oven preheated to 180°C (350°F, Gas mark 4) for 20 minutes until springy to touch.

Allow the cake to cool for a few minutes before turning it out onto a wire rack lined with a tea towel so as not to leave an

MAKING ROSE-WATER GLACÉ ICING

Glacé icing is one of the most popular and simplest of all cake coverings. By replacing the warm water normally used with a flower water you can make glacé icing extra delicious.

Ingredients
250g (9oz/1¾ cup) icing sugar
2-3 tblsp of rose water

Method
Sieve the icing sugar into a bowl; this will help to prevent the icing becoming lumpy. Gradually mix the rose water into the sugar. If you want to ice both the top and the sides of a cake, the icing should be thick enough to coat the back of a spoon. You will need less rose water if you want to cover just the top of the cake.

A cake with a difference to serve on a special occasion: this rose-flavoured cake is covered with rose-water icing. Frosted petals and an edible rose-bud add a graceful finishing touch. (FAR RIGHT)

imprint on your cake. Leave to cool completely.

USING ROSE WATER

Rose water is becoming increasingly widely available and can be found in some supermarkets as well as specialist food stores and chemists. Strengths and flavours vary from brand to brand, so the only sure way of telling whether the amount added to a mixture is correct is to sample it. Orange flower water also can be used to flavour sponge cakes and is particularly good with almond and buttery fillings. It is also readily available.

Instead of the smooth, shiny rose-flavoured glacé icing used in the step by step instructions, you can use richer rose-flavoured whipped cream or buttercream; both of these also can be used as the filling. Whichever covering you choose, it can be coloured with a liquid edible food colouring. Try matching the colouring to the petals, either in a delicate shade of pink if using dark or strongly coloured rose petals, or a deeper shade if using white or pale flowers. For the quickest finish, sprinkle caster sugar over the top of the cake.

FLORAL DECORATION

Although the featured cake is trimmed

DECORATING A CAKE WITH FRESH ROSE PETALS

YOU WILL NEED

 1 *4-5 fragrant edible roses (Rosa gallica)*
 2 *1 rose-bud complete with leaves (for decoration only)*
 3 *150ml (¼pt/⅔ cup) whipping or double cream*
 4 *2-3 tblsp of rose water*
 5 *(2-3oz/2-6 tablespoons) caster sugar*
 6 *2 17.5cm (7in) round sponge cakes*
 7 *1 egg*
 8 *250g (9oz/1¾ cup) icing sugar*
 9 *wire rack*
10 *2 bowls*
11 *whisk*
12 *sieve*
13 *palette knife*
14 *tablespoon*
15 *teaspoon*
16 *greaseproof paper*
17 *weighing scales*

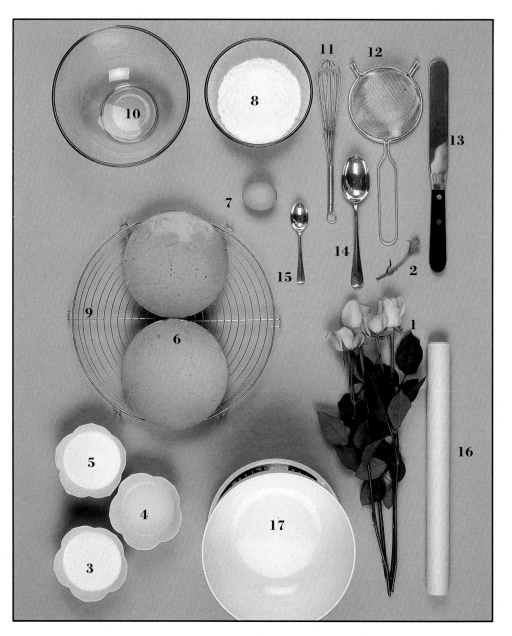

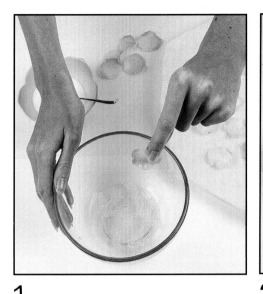

1

2

3

4

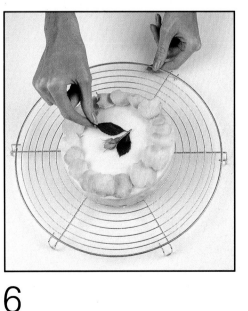

5

6

1 Remove about 20 of the best petals from the roses to decorate the cake. Remove the base of the petals. Beat the white of the egg. Dip the petals into the egg white, allowing the excess liquid to drip off.

2 Measure out about 50g (2oz/ 5 tablespoons) of caster sugar. Sprinkle the egg white-covered petals with caster sugar. Repeat the process on the under-side of the petals. Place the coated petals on a wire rack covered in greaseproof paper to dry. Leave in a warm, draught-free place for 24 hours to harden.

3 Pull off the remaining petals from the roses. Remove the base of the petals as before. Tear up until you have the equivalent of about two heaped tablespoons. Beat the whipping or double cream until it stands in soft peaks. Fold in the petals. Sandwich the cakes together.

4 Sieve 250g (9oz/1¾cup) of icing sugar into a bowl. Little by little, add the rose water to the icing sugar, mixing constantly with a metal spoon. Add sufficient rose water to make a smooth consistency that will spread easily.

5 Place the cake on a wire rack positioned over greaseproof paper to catch any drips. Pour the rose water icing over the top of the cake and spread the icing evenly. Spread the mixture over the sides too. Once the cake is covered, place it in a cool place to let the icing set.

6 When the icing is almost hard, place the reserved frosted petals in a circle around the cake edge so that they overlap slightly. Wash and dry a small rose-bud and position it in the centre of the cake with a couple of rose leaves. Keep the finished cake in the refrigerator until you are ready to serve it.

IMITATION LEAVES

If you do not want to use plant foliage to decorate your cake, try making edible leaves from marzipan or chocolate.

● Lightly knead two or three drops of edible green food colouring into 100g (4oz) of marzipan until it is tinted green. Roll out the marzipan so it is about 7mm (¼in) thick and cut into rose leaf shapes. Lightly mark 'veins' on the leaf with the knife point. Leave to dry.

● To make chocolate leaves, wash and dry a few rose leaves. Melt a small bar of chocolate in a bowl placed over hot water. Use a small paintbrush to coat the under-side of the real rose leaves with an even layer of chocolate. Place on a wire rack to dry, chocolate side uppermost. Once the chocolate has hardened, carefully peel off the real leaf.

Scented pelargonium leaves are baked into a sponge cake for a less formal occasion when you wish to use flowers in cooking. (BELOW)

with frosted rose petals, you can create a spontaneous floral decoration using fresh flowers or petals scattered on top. However you decide to use them, use flowers that are perfect and are free from insects and insecticide and herbicide sprays.

If you are using flowers from the garden, try to gather the roses on a dry day. If the blooms are not to be used immediately, keep them fresh by standing the stems in water until they are required. Alternatively, keep loose petals fresh in a sealed polythene bag placed in the refrigerator. Leave decorating the cake until the last moment and always handle the buds and petals with care.

EDIBLE FLOWERS

If you choose to eat the fragrant roses, use the edible variety *Rosa gallica*. Flower varieties other than roses can be used to decorate cakes, provided they are edible. Suitable edible flowers that look and taste delicious include: elderflowers, violets, primroses, pansies, carnations, nasturtiums, daisies, camomile, hollyhocks, freesias and sprays of almond blossom.

It also is advisable to use leaves that are edible. Rose geranium would be most appropriate for rose cake. Lemon geranium or herb leaves also can be used, but try not to use extremely pungent foliage, especially of the strongly flavoured varieties such as rosemary, otherwise the foliage will mask the delicate floral flavours. If you use non-edible leaves and flowers to decorate your cake, remember to remove them before the cake is eaten.

You can, however, bake a deliciously different cake using pelargonium leaves. Use the same basic whisked sponge-cake recipe as for the petal-decorated cake, just press the leaves into the bottom of the tin when baking so that when the cake is turned out they are decorating the top of the cake.

Alternatively, you can make edible leaves from marzipan or chocolate (see box for details).

When suitable fresh flowers are not available, you can use flowers moulded from marzipan or fondant – available from good confectioners – or frosted flowers or petals.

This cake is best eaten on the day it is made, when it is fresh. However, it can be kept for a day or overnight if stored in an air-tight container in the refrigerator.

FLOWERS FOR A TEA-TRAY

A SMALL BUNCH OF FLOWERS ON A TRAY SHOWS A VISITOR JUST HOW MUCH YOU CARE

When entertaining friends for afternoon tea or preparing a breakfast tray for a guest or relation, make the tray look extra special by adding a small, simple bunch of fresh flowers. Your guests are certain to appreciate this personal touch.

The size and colour of the tray and the material it is made of – whether it's silver, pine, Japanese-style lacquer, tin, modern black ash or chrome – should all be taken into consideration before deciding upon the type of flowers to use and the size of the arrangement.

When choosing a suitable vase, make sure that it will fit comfortably on the tray without the flowers dipping into the food, milk jug, or tea cups. Also check that the base of the container holding the flowers is stable and will not slide about or topple over when you carry your tea into the living room. It is a good idea not to fill your vase to the brim to avoid accidental water spillage.

Match the colours and shapes of your flowers to that of your tray and tea set to give a greater sense of unity. For our featured display small, brightly-coloured blue and purple flowers such as grape hyacinths, anemones and violets are matched to the tablecloth and the blue flower pattern on the glazed-pottery tea set and cream-coloured spray carnations complement the tray. By using a matching piece of pottery from the set as a container for the flowers, a strong visual link is created between them. You could use a jug or spare tea cup from the set if you don't own a matching vase, it will look every bit as effective.

Try to avoid using flowers that have a strong scent, as they may taint the flavour of the food and drink. Other flowers that would be ideal for a small tray display include: spray chrysanthemums, alstroemeria (which can be cut down into individual short stems), small roses, single cymbidium orchids, and gypsophila. Mix these florist blooms with flowers from the garden such as pansies and forget-me-nots to create fuller displays.

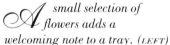

A small selection of flowers adds a welcoming note to a tray. (LEFT)

Romance with Flowers

BRING ROMANCE INTO YOUR LIFE WITH FLOWERS, WHETHER IN
AN ELABORATE BOUQUET OR A SINGLE RED ROSE.

Flowers bring romance to every occasion, whether they are used to fill a party venue with colour and fragrance or carried as small bunches and worn in lapels. Indeed, memorable events such as weddings and christenings, engagement and anniversary parties are considered incomplete without the welcome addition of flowers.

The romantic associations of flowers lie not only in their visual appeal but also in their symbolic meaning. When suitors in Elizabethan times found it hard to express their feelings in words, a whole language was devised in which almost every known flower carried a special message. The

Victorians revived this charming custom of 'saying it with flowers' and compiled comprehensive dictionaries which listed each plant type and its hidden meaning.

THE LANGUAGE OF FLOWERS

Some of the romantic language of flowers still lives on in popular plant names today. Forget-me-not is an obvious entreaty spoken straight from the heart; love-lies-bleeding signifies the sadness of a broken romance; honesty is a clear statement of intentions; and Virginia creeper is symbolised by the phrase, 'I cling to you'. Love-in-a-mist may be so called because both the blue and pink flowers and, later in the season, the striped seedheads are encased in a mesh of tendrils. To Victorians, however, the name had less to do with the plant's appearance and more to do with a state of mind. It signified 'perplexity in love'.

There are other old flower meanings that still have significance today; pansies for thoughts, rosemary for remembrance, four-leafed clover for luck, ivy for fidelity (from the plant's tendency to cling) and orange blossom for purity. None, however, equals the popular perception of a red rose to convey the message of true love.

ROSES FOR LOVERS
Whenever a floral statement of affection is sent from one person to another, it is highly likely that the gift will be a single red rose-bud (which signifies young love)

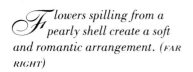

A bunch of flowers is always an appreciated token of admiration. (RIGHT)

Flowers spilling from a pearly shell create a soft and romantic arrangement. (FAR RIGHT)

A simple vase of spring forget-me-nots offers an instantly recognizable message straight from the heart and brings a splash of colour to a dark kitchen corner. (RIGHT)

or a bouquet of roses. Even when the gift is more enduring – a piece of jewellery for example – there will often be a rose pinned to the packaging to underline the sentiments.

If you have received a gift of roses, you will want to make the flowers into a special arrangement to last as long as possible. Give the roses a new lease of life by re-cutting the stem ends straight away. Use a sharp pair of secateurs to cut the stems at an angle and then make criss-cross cuts in the end with a small knife blade. This enables the flowers to take up water easily. Leave the roses closely wrapped in paper and stand them up to their necks in water in a cool, dark place, for a couple of hours.

ROSES IN ARRANGEMENTS
A single red rose looks most beautiful when displayed in an elegant specimen

vase. A sparkling crystal or glass vase looks particularly romantic. Include a few sprays of the glossy foliage if possible – roses look better set against their own leaves. If this isn't possible, for example, if the foliage was crushed in transit, include two or three sprays of shiny leaves such as camellia, hypericum, rhodo-dendron or ivy. A single red rose looks perfect displayed on a dressing table, a bedside shelf or gracing the table for a candlelit dinner for two.

Another romantic Victorian custom was to display a single red rose as the central feature of an arrangement. Make one yourself by gathering up a handful of flowers in complementary shades of mauve, pink, cream or white such as Virginia stocks, nemesia, annual phlox, border pinks or verbena hybrids. Hold the rose in one hand and add the flowers in colourful rings around it.

Outline the bunch with a collar of leaves, such as frilly-edged lady's mantle foliage, bind the stems and cut them to an even length. Lower it into the daintiest bowl or shallow vase you can find. Even when mixed with such vibrant flowers, the rose will still be the focal point.

A FRAGRANT BOUQUET

A formal style is not in keeping with a soft, romantic rose display. A simple mass of thickly clustered roses is far more appropriate than a formal design. Experiment with a sparkling glass vase of deep red, pale pink and pure white roses nestling among strings of pearls on a bedroom table; or a chunky pottery bowl filled with cabbage-like and wild roses and positioned on a hall table.

CONTAINER CHOICE

The choice of container is all-important when creating a romantic arrangement. Look over your collection of jugs, mugs, vases and glasses and pick out anything unusual. Junk shops often yield decorative but inexpensive treasures.

Glass of all kinds brings a romantic feel to an arrangement. Single drinking glasses look good holding a small bunch of delicate flowers with a tendril of leaves trailing over the rim. A small ball of scrunched-up chickenwire to hold the stems is unlikely to show through cut or moulded glass. If the container is valuable or delicate and risks being scratched or damaged by rough-edged wire, it is best to use the stems themselves to hold others in place. Stem-holding devices are not necessary for tall, narrow-necked glass containers such as wine carafes. These vessels display tall, straight-stemmed flowers to perfection. A vase of sweet-scented white lilies or roses, alstroemeria or nerines and delicate gypsophila makes a lovely dressing-table accessory, particularly if placed in front of a mirror.

Heart-shaped candles, coloured tapers and bows on the chairs – the perfect setting for pots of love-in-a-mist, sweet peas, aquilegia and Canterbury bells. (BELOW)

ATTRACTIVE SEA SHELLS

A hint of mother-of-pearl makes any container look extra special. A pearl necklace twirling around the foot or tied around the neck of a glass container also creates a romantic impression. Pearlised glasses glint from pink to blue to green and cream as the light changes. This allows you to select flowers in any one or a blend of the pearly colours to match the container. For all their brittle and craggy exterior, shells of all kinds also have romantic associations. They make delightful accessories to flower arrangements, transforming a simple bunch of fresh flowers into a thoughtful still-life composition.

ARRANGING WITH SHELLS

A pretty shell with a deep aperture can be transformed into a charming container. Wedge a block of soaked foam into the neck, and arrange an overspilling, trailing collection of foliage and flowers. Choose misty-blue sweet peas, silvery statice, snippings of Chinese bellflower, perennial flax, gypsophila and long, slender stems of variegated periwinkle or small ivy leaves. The choice of flower colours will depend on your own room scheme but muted and pastel colours are more flattering to the pearlised shell interiors.

Try to fit the shell with foam and

The ultimate romantic flowers. A shallow bowl packed with cream and red roses makes an intimate setting for a cosy evening for two. (ABOVE)

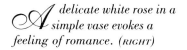

A delicate white rose in a simple vase evokes a feeling of romance. (RIGHT)

arrange the flowers in a way that reveals some of the mother-of-pearl surface. Check daily that the foam is moist. There is not likely to be enough space around the foam to pour water directly into the shell opening. Instead, lift the foam wedge out completely and stand it in a bowl of water until it is fully saturated, then put it carefully back into the shell.

CANDLES AND FLOWERS

Candles and flowers make a perfect partnership, even in summer. Display a plate of scented nightlights in pale apricot, peach, lemon and pink alternating with tiny flowers in spice jars or egg cups.

The chubby shapes and tiny flickering flames of nightlights look romantic and pretty however they are displayed.

Arrange them in a heart shape on a shallow dish – you need eight to make the outline – and scatter a few fresh or dried flowerheads around them.

The combination of hearts and flowers and fluttering candles calls for a celebration drink. The pop of a bottle of champagne comes instantly to mind. Another inspired idea is to put your flowers, such as long-stemmed irises or roses into champagne glasses to create the perfect combination of romance and flowers.

For a romantic drink idea, fill the prettiest bowl you can find with a pink wine cup – blend sparkling wine, lemonade and grenadine sirop and then float the bowl with pink rose petals, geranium flowers, apple blossom or clove carnation petals.

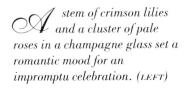

A stem of crimson lilies and a cluster of pale roses in a champagne glass set a romantic mood for an impromptu celebration. (LEFT)

Valentine's Day Arrangement

An occasion like Valentine's Day gives you the perfect opportunity to treat yourself, and a loved one, to an intimate dinner for two. This lovely fresh flower arrangement will get the evening off to the best possible start, and it's a thoughtful way of showing off the flowers given to you for Valentine's Day.

It's an unusual, two-tiered display, with a central vertical feature of long-stemmed red roses, and a low 'all-round' base of foliage, tulips and gypsophila. The design effectively combines two approaches; the lower section is constructed according to traditional guidelines while the starkly upright roses add a distinctly modern touch.

CHOOSING THE FLOWERS

Long-stemmed red roses form the upper focal point. Although in many displays you can get by with less expensive, short-stemmed, sweetheart-type roses, here, stem-length is important, and are worth paying a little extra for. Red roses are the perfect colour for Valentine's Day, but you could use deep or pale-pink, apricot, peach or creamy white roses instead. Yellow roses have a coolness of colour which is not really in keeping with the spirit of the occasion, though they might be just right for another evening.

If possible, buy the roses in fairly tight bud the day before you need them. Condition the roses as soon as you get them home. Cut a tiny bit off the stems, to prevent air locks from forming, then put them in a bucket or tall container of water in a cool place overnight. Conditioning is doubly important for this display, as the stems and flowers have to stand upright, and if not full of water, they will droop.

BEAUTIFUL BLOOMS

Pale-pink tulips are the main flowers in the 'lower' display. Because it can some-times be difficult to find tulips in the shops that are anything more than buds showing colour, look around a few days before the big day, and buy tulip buds if necessary, in advance, so they'll be fully coloured when you need them. Keep them somewhere light and warmish, but not hot as they will dry out.

You could use deep-pink tulips instead, or the beautiful pink parrot tulips, if you can get them, tinged with green and red. Matching the red of roses and tulips is tricky, and if one is slightly more orange than the other, the effect can be unpleasant. You could, however, reverse the display colours, and use pink long-stemmed roses along with red tulips.

Because the appearance of tulip and rose foliage is so important in this design, check that the leaves are in perfect condition before buying. Avoid any that are limp, torn, brown or shrivelled round the edges. Long-stemmed roses are usually sold by the stem, so you can easily inspect the leaves. Bunches of tulips in tight transparent wrappers may prove a bit more difficult to examine, but a helpful florist will probably check them for you.

Dyed pink gypsophila is used in its usual 'filler' role. Though your florist is more likely to stock this speciality around Valentine's day than at any other time of year, you might still need to order it in advance. At a pinch, white gypsophila could also be used, in its large or small-flowered varieties. Dyed gypsophila is more expensive than white, but you can dry it when you take apart the arrangement, once the other fresh flowers have faded. You can also do the same with any roses that wilt while still in bud – just cut off the wet ends of the stems, and hang the roses upside down in a warm, dry and airy spot. If the roses have opened and faded, they will be unsuitable for drying and should be discarded.

This elegant and unusual two-tiered display makes a memorable and romantic dining table centrepiece for a Valentine's Day dinner for two. Long-stemmed roses, tulips, gypsophila, ferns and euphorbia foliage are combined to create a delicate, feminine-looking arrangement, perfect for the occasion. (RIGHT)

Romantic red roses and tulips add extra romance to any Valentine's Day celebration. (RIGHT)

FERNS AND FOLIAGE

Leatherleaf fern is imported, but you could substitute the native male fern, *Dryopteris filix-mas*, to which the leatherleaf fern is related; or the evergreen hard fern, *Blechnum spicant*, which also has tough, leathery fronds, and tolerates dry air.

The euphorbia, *E. marginata*, has white flowers, but they are so tiny that they make no impact. Its green and white variegated foliage and leaf-like bracts, however, are strikingly fresh-looking, and especially attractive used all together, as here. It's a hardy annual garden plant, known as 'snow on the mountain'. Its flowers appear in late summer, so for Valentine's Day, you'll have to buy imported stems from florist shops.

CHOOSING THE CONTAINER

As the sides of the container will be visible below the display, it is important to use an attractive one. A low, round, straight-sided china dish is used, about 20cm (8in) across. Our featured container is white, but it could be pink or red, though matching it to the red of fresh flowers can be difficult!

The container should be deep enough to keep the foam block in position. Alternatively, you could use a shallow wicker basket sprayed white (use car enamel aerosols available from car accessory shops). Remember to allow time for the paint to dry, and line the basket with polythene or kitchen plastic wrap before use.

CHOOSING THE FOLIAGE

Leatherleaf fern and euphorbia foliage supplement the rose and tulip leaves. Leatherleaf fern, *Dryopteris erythrosora*, has shiny, stiff, dark-green fronds. The fronds are tougher than many other, more delicate ferns (hence its common name), but it still needs frequent misting to retain its freshness. It's also a good idea to totally submerge the ferns in water for several hours, or overnight, before use to make certain that they last for as long as possible. Buy a large bunch of 20-30 fronds, and keep them cool and damp until you're ready to begin your display and the arrangement will last that bit longer.

REMOVING TULIP STEMS FROM LEAVES

You can often make good use of cut-off tulip leaves, either with their own flowers or in another display. When you cut the flowers short, as here, stumpy stems remain attached to the pairs of leaves. Don't use scissors to cut away the rest of the stems: they won't reach deep enough, and you'll be left with a shorter, but just as unattractive stump. Instead, bend back the leaves as far as they will go, then cleanly break off the stem with your fingers, and you're left with a neat edge.

CHOOSING THE SETTING

A dining-room table is the obvious spot for this display, and if you have a pink tablecloth and napkins, this is the time to bring them out. If your tablecloth is white, you could buy inexpensive pink or red paper napkins, to reinforce the colour scheme and mood. Though tall flower arrangements on dining room tables are not usually recommended, this one is narrow enough to look round.

If you have young children you might want to move the display to a safer spot on a sideboard in the dining room, or corner table in the living room, when Valentine's Day is over. Two pairs of hands are better than one for this task, to prevent the roses from toppling over.

ALTERNATIVE ARRANGEMENTS

In the less formal Valentine's Day arrangement below, a round wicker basket with quite a high handle has been used. Before adding the flowers, the basket must be lined with thick polythene

REVIVING WILTED ROSES

Hybrid tea roses are liable to wilt and bend just under the flowerhead even though the flower still has plenty of life left. This is usually due to an air blockage in the stem, which prevents water from reaching the flowerhead. Roses can be revived to stand upright again by recutting the stems (ideally under water) and completely submerging the flowers and stems in water for several hours.

to make it watertight. Add a block of pre-soaked florist's foam which comes about 2.5cm (1in) above the basket. This ensures that stems can be put into the side of the foam as well as the top so some stems can flow down in a graceful line. When you work on this display, bear in mind that the design will be seen from all angles.

Mixed roses in pastel shades are arranged with ivy sprays in a simple wicker basket. The handle is twisted with trails of ivy which give the display a softer, more romantic silhouette. (LEFT)

FLOWER LANGUAGE

Flowers have always had a language of their own, and over the centuries different meanings have been attributed to them.

The flowers featured in the main arrangement were not only chosen for their decorative qualities but also for their particular romantic message. The message of love and affection has always been expressed through gifts of red roses, and tulips also carry the same meaning. What better way of creating a romantic atmosphere than with a quiet dinner for two and beautiful flowers!

CREATING A FRESH VALENTINE'S DAY DISPLAY

YOU WILL NEED

1 *12 red roses*
2 *6-8 euphorbia stems*
3 *10-12 tulips*
4 *bunch of dyed pink gypsophila*
5 *20-30 fern fronds*
6 *block of florist's foam*
7 *floristry knife*
8 *low china container*

1

2

3

4

5

6

1 Soak a foam block then cut it to snuggly fit the container standing about 3cm (1½in) above the rim. Cut off the tips of the stem ends of 20-30 fern fronds. Push the stalks into the sides of the foam block, angling the fronds downwards. Overlap the fronds, and insert them to form a bushy collar around the foam.

2 Shorten the rose stems to 30-45cm (12-18in), cutting the stems at an angle. Insert the stem deeply into the foam block. Place the tallest stems in the centre, the shorter ones clustered around them. Insert the roses close together, to form a tight mass, but splay them out.

3 Cut off the leafy tops from 6-8 euphorbia stems, Euphorbia bleeds milky latex when cut, so insert it at once into the foam, to block the flow. Insert the euphorbia tight against the foam block, to make a dense, frilly covering of foliage from the fern collar to the base of the roses.

4 Cut the stems of 10-12 tulips back to 7.5cm (3in), reserving the tulip foliage for use later. Insert the tulip stems in between the euphorbia foliage. The tulip stems should be hidden by the foliage, and the flowerheads should stand a little above the surrounding leaves.

5 Cut the gypsophila, to about 7.5cm (3in) long. Bunch several sprigs in your hand, then insert among the tulips and euphorbia. Place the gypsophila horizontally around the sides of the block, gradually angling the bunches upwards.

6 Break off the reserved headless tulip stalks so that just the curly leaves remain (see box). Insert the leaves as close as you can at the base of the bare rose stems, entwining some of the leaves around the stems.

STEP *by* STEP

Everlasting Valentine's Display

Traditionally, red roses have been regarded as the Valentine's Day gift and here is a new and innovative arrangement for this romantic occasion. Our heart-shaped basket contains dried red roses to symbolise lasting love and affection. Dried lavender lends fragrance and colour, and white gypsophila a lacy elegance to the finished display.

This simple arrangement will complement other decorative objects on a small coffee or dressing table, but will also hold its own on a plain wooden table top where the basket blends in subtly with the colour of the wood.

If you want to be less conventional, you can use your favourite flowers from the wide range of dried ones available in the shops for a very personal message, but keep the flowerheads you choose small to achieve a similar neatly compact, pincushion effect.

CHOOSING THE ROSES
Long-stemmed roses are used here but you can save money by choosing short-stemmed, sweetheart roses, since the stems are cut off anyway for the final display.

Dried roses are only slightly more expensive than fresh roses but you can always make a small saving and dry your own at home. As a further economy, save the cut-off stems and dried leaves to add body to another dried-flower display you can do at a different time. The beauty of using dried materials is that they never go to waste as they can so easily be stored for a later date.

Deep wine-red roses are chosen for this display, but, on a softer note, you could choose dried peach-coloured roses, pale or deep pink, apricot or yellow roses depending on personal taste and the colour scheme of your room's decor and furnishings.

An especially charming choice for Valentine's Day would be the dried sweetheart rose which is white with petals edged in deep pink, but you'd have to order them well in advance from your florist. Unfortunately, you won't be able to find pure red dried roses, as they always dry out several shades darker than their natural colour.

On a budget, you could substitute pale pink or red helichyrsums, for the roses – the effect would be just as charming. Be careful when choosing red helichyrsums, as some of them have a distinctly orange tinge. Hold the helichyrsums close to the light – ideally look at them in natural daylight – to identify and separate the orange-tinged flowers from the blue-red ones.

ADDING A FRAGRANT TOUCH
In this display, lavender provides the fragrance that dried roses lack. Lavender grown and harvested for floristry comes in just one colour, so you don't have to worry about making the right choice!

If you are unable to find dried lavender in the shops, you could use lavender pot-pourri instead. Sprinkle the pot-pourri over the foam block so it is concealed once the roses and gypsophila have been positioned.

White gypsophila is used as the filler in this arrangement, and adds a delicate lightness to the rather heavy colour of the deep-red roses. Equally, the lacy quality of gypsophila is a bit like the old lace that was sometimes used to decorate Victorian Valentine's Day cards.

CHOOSING THE CONTAINER
A woven twig heart-shaped basket, 7.5cm (3in) deep, is used for this display; your florist should be able to order a similar

Almost jewel-like in quality – the roses could be rubies and the gypsophila pearls – this heart-shaped basket is a perfect everlasting Valentine's Day gift. (FAR RIGHT)

one from a wholesale supplier. If not, don't worry – there are a variety of alternatives. For the two or three weeks leading up to Valentine's Day, all manner of heart-shaped baskets appear on the market. Empty heart-shaped containers are also sold in gift shops, department stores and basket shops.

Obviously, a heart-shaped basket is perfect for Valentine's Day, but you could build up the display in a round, oval, hexagonal, square or rectangular container. Metallic-covered, heart-shaped cardboard boxes, such as those used for chocolates, are also a possible substitute, provided they are deep enough to hold the dry foam block.

CHOOSING THE SETTING

This traditionally feminine display would look perfect on a dressing table, bedside table or even on a wide windowsill. You could also display it vertically on a bookshelf or in a glass cabinet: the latter will help to keep it dust free. Make sure it is firmly supported, though, so it doesn't topple over or slide down.

CARING FOR THE DISPLAY

Sooner or later the volatile oils of lavender will dissipate, and the fragrance of the display diminish. When this happens, you can refresh it by adding a couple of drops of oil of lavender, available from beauty shops and some chemists.

CREATING AN EVERLASTING BASKET DISPLAY

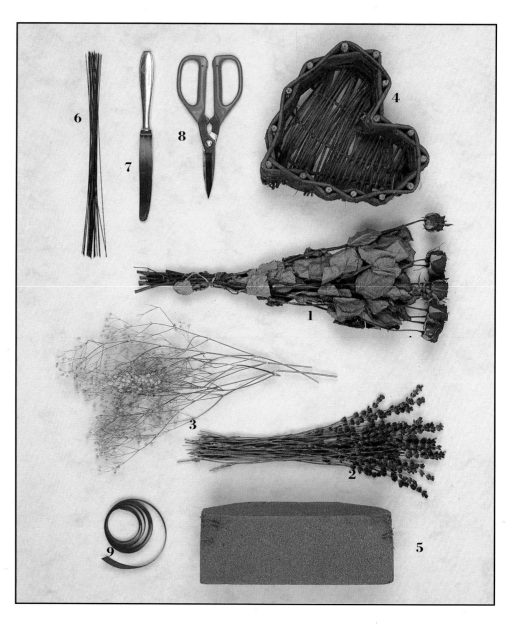

YOU WILL NEED

1 *25-30 dried red roses*
2 *25-30 dried lavender sprigs*
3 *1 small bunch of dried white gypsophila*
4 *woven twig heart-shaped basket*
5 *block of dry florist's foam*
6 *light gauge stub wire*
7 *knife*
8 *floristry scissors*
9 *red ribbon (optional) quick-drying glue*

1

2

3

4

5

6

1 Cut and shape the dry foam block to fit snugly into the basket. Use the base of the basket as a template. Cut around the outline with a knife. The foam block should be two-thirds the height of the basket so the tops of the flowers sit above the rim.

2 Carefully cut the lavender stems 2cm (¾in) below the base of each flower spike. Make into clumps of two to three flower spikes each and insert into the foam block, pushing the stems in as far as the base of the flower spikes. Position the clumps evenly.

3 Using sharp scissors, cut the stems of two bunches of roses to 2cm (¾in) below the flowerheads. Insert the roses individually and evenly spaced apart in the foam. Be careful when inserting the roses not to dislodge or damage the lavender.

4 Cut off tiny sprigs from the top of a small bunch of dried gypsophila, leaving about 2cm (¾in) of stem on each sprig. Using light gauge wire, wire up into little florets of three to four sprigs each. Cut the stub wire to 2cm (¾in) so that the floret heads of gypsophila stand above the rim of the basket.

5 Carefully insert the wired-up sprigs of dried gypsophila between the roses and the lavender. Allow some gypsophila to overhang the basket, softening the outline.

6 Decorate the basket with ribbon as an optional extra. Cut the ribbon to three to four times the length of the heart and fold in half. Use glue to fix the fold to the pointed tip of the basket, midway down. Bring the two ends tightly round the sides and into the central recess. Use hairpin-shaped wire to secure. Cut the two streamers into V-shaped 'fish tails'.

Blending in subtly with the polished wood surface of the handsome dressing table, this woven twig, flower-filled basket is brilliantly offset by gleaming glass and silver. The lacy white elegance of the gypsophila echoes the openwork lace coverings. (RIGHT)

MENDING BROKEN ROSE STEMS

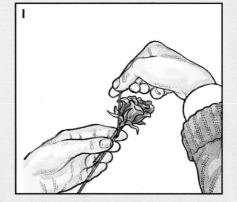

1 To mend a broken rose head, take a length of stub wire and hold it up against the base of the rose head.

2 Take a piece of fine reel wire and wind it round the stem and stub wire to bind the two together. Keep winding until you reach the end of the stub wire. Cut it off and secure.

3 Finish off by binding the wire stems with green florist's tape. In this display, the wire stems are hidden by the gypsophila so this is optional.

THE LANGUAGE OF FLOWERS

Get to know the language of flowers – often, it speaks louder than words.

Giving a gift of flowers, specially chosen for their particular meaning, is a charming way to express an emotion – whether love and admiration, joy or sorrow. You may not know it, but if you give someone a bunch of pinks you are saying 'I love you'. And if the flowers are French marigolds you are declaring 'I'm jealous'.

You may not know it, but if you give someone a bunch of pinks you are saying 'I love you'. And if the flowers are French marigolds you are declaring 'I'm jealous'.

For centuries, certain meanings have been attributed to flowers, and during the Victorian era in particular, they were a favourite means of sending special messages.

This method of communication is not without pitfalls, however; some flowers have more than one meaning and the meaning can change quite drastically according to the colour of the flower. For instance, red chrysanthemums mean 'love' while yellow means 'slighted love'.

And it was not just the choice of flowers that could 'speak' in Victorian times, how they were presented was also significant. A single flower positioned to the right meant that the message referred to the giver, but if the flower pointed to the left the message was directed to the receiver.

Not only could declarations be made and questions asked through the language of flowers, there was also a 'code' for answering. If the response was 'yes', the recipient would touch the flower to their lips, but if it was 'no', a petal was plucked and allowed to fall to the floor.

This delightful, old-fashioned custom is ripe for revival, and there is more than one way to 'say it with flowers'. As well as giving a bouquet or a bunch of flowers, gifts can be decorated with fresh, dried, artificial or embroidered flowers specially selected for their meaning.

So that friends will know there is more to your choice and arrangement of flowers than pure decoration, and to ensure that your thoughts and messages are appreciated, it's important to let them into the 'secret'. After all, if they are unaware that you are saying something the gesture is wasted.

The message could be included on the gift itself; for example, by embroidering it on a flower-filled cushion, nightdress case or place mats. If this is impractical, the message can be written on gift tags and greeting cards decorated with pressed, dried, drawn or painted flowers. Or, to make it as clear as possible, it could be written on an accompanying, flower-decorated card.

So that friends can return the gesture, you might like to make up a list of flowers and their meanings and present them as a 'dictionary of flowers'. Written on an attractive card and decorated with a selection of pressed flowers, this would make a charming and unusual gift.

Here are the meanings of some of the most common flowers:

Almond blossom – hope
Amaryllis – pride, splendid beauty
Anemone – forsaken
Bell flower – gratitude
Red carnation – alas for my poor heart
Striped carnation refusal
Red chrysanthemum – love
Daisy – innocence
Forget-me-not – fidelity, true love
Scarlet geranium – comfort
Honeysuckle –devotion
Yellow jasmine – happiness, grace and elegance
Jonquil – I desire a return of affection
Marigold – joy
Michaelmas daisy – farewell
Mignotte – your qualities are supreme
Peony – bashfulness
Red poppy – consolation
Rose-bud – pure and lovely
Yellow rose – infidelity
Snapdragon – 'no'
Snowdrop – hope, consolation
Wallflower – fidelity in adversity
Zinnia – thoughts of absent friends

Weddings and Anniversaries

CAREFUL PLANNING IS THE KEY TO ARRANGING SUCCESSFUL
FLOWERS FOR BIG EVENTS FROM WEDDINGS TO CHRISTENINGS.

Arranging flowers for a wedding occasion
is a test for any arranger's skill and
creativity. Flowers will play a significant
role throughout the day. From the bridal
bouquet which must perfectly complement the bride's dress to the church
flowers and flowers that decorate and
enhance the reception hall – it is up to the
arranger to make the occasion just that bit
more special.

It is the bride's day, and the flowers she
and her attendants will carry and wear are
the most important of all. The colour and
style of the bridal flowers will set the
theme for those used to decorate the
church and reception hall, providing a
focal point from which all the other
flowers take their cue.

If, for example, the bride decides to
carry a bouquet of pale green orchids,
white verbena and peach roses, her
choice will determine the colours and the
style of the other wedding flowers. Her
selection of traditional and elegant flowers
may suggest arrangements with the style
and grace associated with symmetrical
pedestals, triangular and other regular
and recognised shapes.

If, on the other hand, the bride chooses
a casual display of pale-blue, lace-cap
hydrangeas blended with pink and blue
cornflowers and a cloud of lime-green
lady's mantle, this will call for a much
less formal approach. The flowers in
church and at the reception could be more
'countrified', comprising pretty hoops,
circlets, ribbon-hanging spheres packed
with pink and blue blossoms, and trailing
garlands of soft greenery.

Flowers for a wedding must look cool
and elegant even on the hottest of days.
Those which last especially well include
carnations, spray carnations, single
chrysanthemums, orchids, freesias, lilies,
stephanotis, rosebuds and half-open
roses, gypsophila and lady's mantle.

THE RIGHT PREPARATION

Take the earliest opportunity to go along
to the church and the reception hall with
the bride so that you can plan the flowers
together. Ask the vicar, priest or rector for
permission to arrange flowers in the
church, and check what are the particular
customs and preferences. At certain fest-
ivals in the church year, you may not be
allowed to place flowers on the altar, and
some churches do not allow the font to be
decorated in any way.

It is also tactful to ask the flower-rota
organisers if you can relieve them of their
duties for the day. They will be able to
show you what pedestals and other suitable containers are available at the
church. You can then plan to hire any
others you may need from the florist where
you buy your flowers.

Make a note of all the relevant dimensions, the colour and type of the backgrounds, the direction of the light and any
other factors which will affect the way the
flower arrangements will be viewed. Go
through each stage in the proceedings,
from the bride's arrival and the walk up
the aisle to the ceremony at the altar steps
and the signing of the register in the

*The bride's radiance is
further enhanced by
flowers; from the magnificent
bouquet to splendid church
flowers. (FAR RIGHT)*

vestry, and concentrate your arrangements on those areas.

POSITIONING THE DISPLAYS

It might be possible to greet the bridal party and guests with a pedestal of flowers in the porch – the actual size of the area and the degree of protection from the wind may be deciding factors – or to place a basket of flowers on benches on each side of the outer door. If this is not practicable, you can move your welcoming arrangement just inside the church door, with a pedestal placed to one side of the entrance or a display on the hymn-book table.

The altar steps, where the marriage service is usually held, are the main focus of attention. You may like to place a pair of matching pedestals on either side. Instead, there may be a pair of slim tables or stools which could support two displays that can be seen by the rest of the congregation.

Make a note of the colour and type of the material that forms the background – whether it is a painted or carved wood screen, silk drapes or a stone wall. This will determine the outline material you choose for the floral designs. In general terms, the fussier or more complicated the background, the more clear-cut should be the outline of the arrangement. Give the design more prominence by using branches of breech, lime or oak foliage to determine the height and width of the arrangements and to frame the flowers.

AISLE DISPLAYS

The bride may have planned on having the pew ends, or at least those of the rows likely to be occupied by guests, decorated with flowers to create a floral avenue on her walk up the aisle. This is a lovely idea, and one which gives as much pleasure to the guests as it does to the bridal group.

Simple bunches of flowers look attractive displayed in this way, the stalks cut short and tied with ribbon bows. Design them flat on a table top, with a backing of leaves to protect and frame the flowers.

Place the longest, most slender and tapering materials in the centre to avoid a heavy look. Trails of small variegated ivy, willow or similar foliage have a dainty and natural appearance. Arrange the flowers in graduated lengths, each row of flower-heads neatly concealing the stems of the layer before.

Bind the stems with raffia and leave the arranged flowers in water until the last possible moment. Wrap the stems in damp tissues, then in foil (to protect the pew ends) and bind them round with ribbon. The flowers will then stay looking fresh and elegant during and after the ceremony.

Arranging the pew end designs in soaked foam ensures a constant supply of water to the flowers. You can use a slice of foam wrapped carefully and closely in foil, but there is always a danger of water seepage through the holes made by inserting the stems. An easier and neater method is to buy a packet of pre-formed rectangular plastic pew-end holders from a florist. They are the right size to take a slice cut from a foam block and they even have a handle, which will make fixing to the pew easy. Give the foam a good soaking in water and secure it firmly in the holder with a criss-cross of adhesive tape so that it is stable enough to receive the flowers.

AN INFORMAL LOOK

For a country-style effect, decorate the pew ends with circlets of flowers, leaves and ribbons. To make the frame, tie a handful of supple broom, willow or clematis twigs into a circle. Alternatively, bend wire coat-hangers into circles and bind on handfuls of sphagnum moss with raffia taken round the hoop. Use a roll of fine wire and bind on a covering of light textured leaves such as sprays of willow or asparagus fern. Do not use heavy evergreen leaves or they will dominate the design. Then wire on individual flowers by a short stem such as lilies, roses,

A stunning display of spider, spray and bloom chrysanthemums, complemented by aucuba foliage and beech leaves on the turn. Displayed in a copper urn, they welcome the bride with a flood of warm autumn sunlight. (LEFT)

Cool white lilies, feathery dill and Ammi majus are combined to produce this informal, country style display, arranged in a large pottery jug and positioned in a shaded church window. (FAR LEFT)

carnations or honeysuckle and bunches of small flowers such as cornflowers and matricaria. Spray the flowers with a fine mist of cool water and keep in a cool, dark place until needed. Twine narrow ribbons in complementary colours around the circles just before putting them in place.

WINDOW FRAMING

Church windows provide inspirational settings for flower arrangements and you might decide to decorate at least those closest to the heart of the ceremony. Remember to measure not only the dimensions of the windows, but the depth of the sill. Some can be surprisingly narrow and have space for only the most shallow baking dish or plastic box as a container for the foam.

When planning a display for a window, make sure that it is large enough to hold its own against the scale of the window, which will effectively serve as a frame.

For this reason a central design may be out of the question, and an arrangement with tall upright branches and long side trails nestling in one corner of the frame would be more suitable.

Also consider the aspects of the windows. If those on one side are likely to be bathed in strong sunlight, then try not to use a colour scheme which is principally white or cream. If such a scheme is unavoidable, blend some mid-toned foliage and flowers in a deeper shade to avoid a bleached-out look.

LEAFY GARLANDS

Garlands or swags of leaves and flowers are traditional decorations for both the church and the wedding reception. You can wind a garland around upright pillars in the church or fix one over an archway to emphasise a good architectural feature. Leafy ribbons wound round the tent poles of a marquee also make an attractive

A simple floral design in the vestry completes the setting for the signing of the register. The glass jar can be arranged with flowers which match exactly those carried by the bride. (RIGHT)

feature. Draw attention to the bridal table, buffet table or wedding cake stand by decorating it with a leafy swag.

All you need to make a garland is a length of thick cord, trails of covering leaves, flowers and a roll of fine wire. Measure the cord accurately. If the swag is to decorate the vertical fall of a tablecloth, don't forget to allow for it to be looped up in the centre. You can use any leaves that combine long-lasting quality with a light appearance.

Variegated ivy, asparagus fern or smilax (*Asparagus asparagoides*) which you can order from the florist are all suitable. Place the leaf sprays against the cord and bind them on with wire. Spray the leaves with water and keep the garland in a cool place as close as possible to the event until required.

THE BRIDE'S TABLE

The flowers arranged for the bride's table at the reception are the most important. It is best to make the designs both simple and elegant. Keep them small and low, so that all eyes can be on the bride, and avoid using over-bright or very dark flowers as these are not suitable types of flower for this occasion.

A pair of silver goblets bubbling over with cream lilies and pink roses, a crystal bowl of golden alstroemeria, freesias and rose-buds, a shallow basket with a long, low horizontal design of pastel pink paeonies, sweet peas and silver foliage – whatever your choice, the design will play an important part in enhancing a memorable occasion.

ADVANCE PLANNING

With so many different ideas and exciting possibilities for wedding flowers, you will need to plan each stage carefully. It is a good idea to make rough sketches of your main arrangements, making a note of each flower type. Prepare all the containers well in advance, fitting them with foam or scrunched up chicken wire and taping it into position.

Condition all foliage and flowers the day before you arrange them. The only flowers which are likely to wilt are those that were selected as an afterthought and were not given a long drink before you arranged them in the foam.

Leave the composition of the arrangements as late as you possibly can and spray them regularly. If you arrange flowers in the church or hall overnight, give them a last-minute check and, if possible, a final spray just before the event.

This formal, triangular arrangement is outlined with oak, beech and hawthorn leaves. The wild ox-eye daisies are blended with yellow roses, spray carnations and pink aquilegia. (ABOVE)

Flowers for the Aisle

As well as having their own special solemnity and beauty, church weddings are the perfect opportunity to create beautifully co-ordinated floral displays. There are many traditional locations for wedding flowers in a church: the altar rail, steps leading to the chancel, windowsills, columns and the main entrance. Pew ends decorated with generously-massed flower displays create a particularly lovely impression and you can make as many pairs of them as you want, according to the size of the church and your budget.

Unlike a display for the home, any floral display in a church has to be substantial to be seen. If you are working on a limited budget, use branches, foliage or flowers from your garden or a friend's garden to keep your florist's bill to a minimum.

Even if you're working to a budget and have to buy all the flowers and foliage from a florist, you can still put on a good show. Under these circumstances it's better to do fewer pew-end displays and make them really generous than to do a number of sparse ones. You could decorate just the pair of pew ends closest to the altar; or in a large church, every second or third pair; the front, middle and back pairs or the front two or three pairs.

The featured pew-end arrangement is teardrop-shaped, like an informal wedding bouquet, and creates a waterfall effect of flowers and foliage. Because you don't want the flowers or branches to catch on the bride's dress or be damaged by guests, keep the display fairly compact, no more than 25cm (10in) deep. This is especially important in the case of a narrow aisle.

DESIGN CONSIDERATIONS
Many churches have pews made of naturally dark or dark-stained wood, and most churches are dimly lit. In this setting, white or pale-pastel flowers show up best, especially from a distance, and of course they should carry through the bridal colour theme. Avoid deep-blue or violet flowers when decorating the church, even if they form part of the bridesmaids' or flower girls' bouquets. Deep blues and violets, and dark reds for that matter, are visually recessive, and tend to look gloomy. They don't photograph well either, which is an important consideration.

Most churches have neutral colour schemes, whether dark wood, stone or rendered and painted walls, so the choice of floral colour scheme depends on personal taste and the colour scheme of the bridal party.

For church flowers, and wedding flowers generally, use a high proportion of open blooms. Wedding displays have a different time scale from ordinary flower arrangements in the home, which are meant to last as long as possible, and are often made up entirely of flowers still in bud. Wedding flowers on the other hand are expected to look beautiful for that day, and that day alone. After the ceremony, some people like to leave the flowers in the church for others to enjoy, or contribute them to a local hospital or old people's home. This is still possible but the arrangements will not last for as long as usual.

PLANNING IN ADVANCE
As soon as the date is set, try to meet whoever is in charge of organising church flowers. You can take measurements and sort out the best time to deliver and arrange the flowers, find out what vases are available, where the water tap is, and so on. Look at the pew ends carefully, since they vary in their design. Some have horizontal indentations through which

This cascading display of pink and white flowers makes the bride's walk up the aisle just that bit more memorable. (FAR RIGHT)

60

securing ribbons can be slotted; with others, the display is hooked over the top.

Always discuss your wedding-flower needs with your florist as soon as the date is set. He or she will be able to tell you what will be available at that time of year, and what the cost is likely to be. They can also arrange to order your flowers early to avoid any last-minute disappointment.

The procedure which most proficient flower-arrangers follow is to make up and position the church flowers the day before the wedding, so they are still fresh on the day. This also allows you to have time to

enjoy yourself without feeling pressured on the wedding day itself. If you are doing all the flowers yourself, try to enlist the help of a friend or two, hopefully with some experience in flower arranging. If you are doing the flowers at home, make sure you have adequate transport to get them to the church on time and in good condition. It is easy to underestimate the amount of space you will need to pack all the arrangements safely into the back of the car. It might be worth hiring an estate car or small van just for the day to be absolutely sure you have enough space.

CREATING A FORMAL PEW-END DISPLAY

YOU WILL NEED

1 *18-20 stems of pink roses*
2 *2-3 stems of gypsophila*
3 *10 stems of cherry blossom*
4 *2-3 stems of pink broom*
5 *16-18 stems of spray
   chrysanthemums*
6 *6-8 stems of laurustinus*
7 *5-6 cyclamen leaves*
8 *3 trailing stems of
   variegated ivy*
9 *foam base for pew ends*
10 *fine stub wires*
11 *scissors*
12 *white ribbon*

1

2

3

4

5

6

1 Soak the foam ball base. Insert three pieces of ivy at least 46cm (18in) long into the base of the foam ball so that they trail downwards. Make a wired bow from the white ribbon and insert it in the middle of the ivy. Wire five or six cyclamen leaves and make a ring of leaves around the foam ball.

2 Cut off the lower flowers from the cherry blossom stems. Leave two stems long and cut the remaining stems in half. Insert the short sprigs into the top of the foam ball in a spiky fan shape. Place the two long stems at the bottom of the ball.

3 Cut several pink broom stems off their main stem to the same length as the ivy. Insert them in the base of the foam so that they spray in a cascading waterfall effect. Be careful when inserting woody stems into foam. If the stems are pushed in too far, the foam will break up.

4 Cut eight or ten open rose stems 20cm (8in) long. Make a fan shape radiating downwards and outwards from the base of the foam ball. Cut the remaining roses shorter and insert in the foam to form a dome shape, covering most of the foam. Place the most open roses in the centre.

5 Cut the spray chrysanthemum stems to the same length as the roses, leaving an upper floret of four or five flowers. Remove most of the leaves from each stem. Place the chrysanthemum florets between the low-lying roses.

6 Cut off little sprigs of laurustinus and intersperse randomly throughout the design, covering any visible foam. Finish off with the gypsophila. As a finishing touch, insert a second wired ribbon bow into the foam at the top of the arrangement.

CHOOSING THE PEW-END FLOWERS

You may want to use the same type of flowers to decorate the pew ends that you use for the bridal bouquet itself. On a budget, however, you may prefer to do without the more expensive lily of the valley and orchids that are usually included in the bouquet.

The main pew-end arrangement shown is made up of a combination of branches from flowering shrubs and herbaceous perennials: cherry blossom, pink broom, single-flowered chrysanthemums, pink roses and gypsophila. The woody branches give length and elegance to the display, the roses and perennial flowers add colour and delicate detail, while the foliage adds bulks, grace and contrasting colour and form to the flowers. Here, ivy, laurustinus and cyclamen leaves are used, but almost any attractive leaves will do, to add the desired effect to this design. The main point to remember is that the chosen leaves must be able to stay fresh-looking for a day or so.

ALTERNATIVE FOUNDATIONS

Florists sell specially-made, half-globe, florist's foam pew-end bases, complete with a clip, as shown. These come in just one size, but by varying the length of the flower and foliage stems, you can create smaller or larger displays in a range of silhouettes, using the same-sized base. If you can't get pew-end bases, florist's foam blocks with plastic backing and pierced handles for hanging are available in a range of sizes.

You can also create lovely, informal pew-end displays without any foundations. Build up an elongated, front-facing, hand-tied bunch, (see box for details). Incorporate plenty of trailing material, and layer the flowers so they don't obscure one another. Cut the stems evenly, then tie securely with a ribbon, making a pretty bow. White ribbon is the best choice to stand out against a dark wooden pew. Tie the flowers to the pew end with more ribbon, and fix another ribbon bow to the back of the pew to finish off.

MAKING AN INFORMAL PEW-END DISPLAY

1 Working with your chosen flowers and foliage, lay the longest, trailing stems, such as bloom or blossom, flat on your working surface.

2 Build up the other flowers and foliage in groups placed in graduating layers, so that they don't obscure one another. Make a focal point of the most open flowers in the centre of the arrangement.

3 Gather the stems together and tie securely with a piece of twine. Cover with a ribbon bow and a long length of ribbon with which to attach the display.

WIRING A RIBBON BOW

Cut the ribbon to a length of 60cm (24in). Holding one end firmly in one hand and leaving a small tail, loop the ribbon into a figure of eight. The size of the loop determines the size of the finished bow. Hold the central point firmly. Make a second figure of eight on top of the first. Continue building up the layers of ribbon loops. Bind a stub wire around the central point to secure the bow. Twist the wire together to form a stem for insertion into the display. Leave the ribbon tails long and trailing or cut short, as required.

T his ribbon-tied bunch of broom, solidaster, freesias, gypsophila and matricaria is the simplest of all possible pew-end displays. Upside-down bunches have no florist's foam to keep them fresh, so choose long-lasting material and condition it well before positioning the display ideally on the morning of the ceremony, rather than the day before. (ABOVE)

STEP *by* STEP

Children's Wedding Displays

A lot of thought and effort goes into the making of bridesmaid's and page boy's costumes, so it seems right to enhance the finished work with inspirational floral designs. We've created a delightful posy and accompanying head-dress for the bridesmaid and a complementary flower-tipped staff for the page boy. Peach chrysanthemums and lilies combine with blue-mauve veronica and white roses and gypsophila to create a soft, pastel effect, but you may want to choose different flowers to complement the textures and

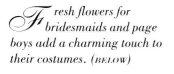

Fresh flowers for bridesmaids and page boys add a charming touch to their costumes. (BELOW)

colours used in the more formal church and reception arrangements. All three displays here are easy and cheap to make, involving simple wiring and taping techniques and relatively few flowers.

If possible, make up your displays on the morning of the event, or the evening before at the earliest. Children may like to take their own flowers home after the event to show their friends, so try to include long-lasting varieties, such as the chrysanthemums and gypsophila shown here.

CHOOSING THE TONAL SCHEME

When choosing the material and colour scheme for your page boy and bridesmaid displays, select one of the lesser featured flowers from the church and reception arrangements and use it to provide a common link. Choose the supporting flowers to give the right effect for the type of display you are making. Head-dresses, for instance, look best when made up of light, delicate flowers, while a bouquet needs a few larger feature flowers to give it an eye-catching centre point.

If the children's outfits are in dark strong colours, choose flowers in clear, pastel shades to stand out clearly. The bridesmaid's dress may be a colour other than white or cream, in which case you can concentrate on finding a few large flowers in a matching colour. Select flowers of a distinctive shape or strong colour to top the page boy's staff in contrast to the soft, rounded shape and pastel shades of the bridesmaid's head-dress and arrangement.

Small children tire quickly after the excitement of the wedding so try to make your design out of light material that is easy to carry. For head-dresses, use lightweight wire and relatively few flowers and avoid flowers with heady scents.

1 Cut two peach-pink chrysanthemums to different lengths and wire into a floret about 20cm (8in) long. Bind the stems with gutta-percha tape. Make up four florets and bind into a bunch with fine reel wire; bind the stems outwards to form a star shape. Leave the wire on the reel and use it to attach three wired and taped ivy leaves to the central stem.

2 Insert four wired florets of gypsophila in between the chrysanthemum heads to build up the height of the display. Wind the fine reel wire around the central stem to secure the florets. Place three wired lily flowers in a line across the centre of the display. Use three wired variegated ivy leaves to encircle the base. Insert two more chrysanthemums to balance the display.

3 Add the blue-mauve veronica flowers at intervals. Insert seven to eight wired stems of daisy chrysanthemums around the lower edges pulling them through from underneath. Insert the six wired spray roses at random. Tape the wired stems together as a single stem and cut to just longer than the width of a child's palm.

This bridesmaid's display combines large peach lilies, white roses and pink and peach chrysanthemums to contrast with delicate florets of gypsophila and spiky veronica heads. (ABOVE)

*T*he spiky elegance
of the page's staff
contrasts with the soft, rounded
shape of the bridesmaid's
display. The veronica spires
emerge from a gypsophila bed
and a horizontal layer of
chrysanthemums and ivy.
(*ABOVE*)

1 Cut a stick of white-painted bamboo to
30cm (12in) or to suit the height of the
page boy. Tape the top end of the stick so
that the wired flowers adhere firmly. Leave
the wire attached to the reel and wind the
end around the top of the stick. Bind the
three wired and taped tops of the blue-
mauve veronica stems securely to the
bamboo with the reel wire.

2 Make up six wired gypsophila florets,
using five to six sprigs for each bunch.
Arrange them as a second layer around the
base of the veronica so that the stems are
covered completely. They should form a
delicate, lacy collar in contrast to the strong
upward form of the veronica spires. Bind
the gypsophila firmly in position.

3 Make a third layer out of five or six
peach-pink daisy chrysanthemums.
Finish off with a closely overlapping layer of
wired variegated ivy leaves to provide a flat
supporting base. Wire the ivy stems to the
stick. Cut all the wired stems to as short a
length as possible and cover them with
tape. Make sure the chrysanthemums and
ivy are visible under the gypsophila.

1 Measure the circumference of the bridesmaid's head and cut a length of thick wire (or two thin wires) to the right length. Cover the wire with gutta-percha tape and use it as the framework of your display. Make a small hook at one end. Assemble a small floret from a wired sprig of gypsophila and two wired peach-pink chrysanthemum heads and tape the stems firmly to the wire with the heads facing outwards, starting at the hook end.

2 Continue down the length of the wire, alternating florets of chrysanthemums and gypsophila with florets of white roses and more gypsophila. Angle the flowers in one direction, spacing them closely together with the head of each bunch immediately below the one above so that the green tape is hidden from view.

3 Finish off at the end with a grouping of gypsophila and white roses. Trim the wire with wire cutters and bend into a small hook. Tape securely over the end. Carefully shape the flower-covered wire into a circle and hook the two ends together. Adjust the length of the wire until the head-dress fits.

A mass of frothy white gypsophila emphasizes the light, airy quality of this simple head-dress and provide a natural base on which to lie the rose and chrysanthemum flowerheads. (ABOVE)

ANNIVERSARY FLOWERS

Celebrate wedding anniversaries by adding traditional gifts to a flower display.

ANNIVERSARY GIFTS

Year	Gift
First	Paper
Second	Cotton
Third	Leather
Fourth	Books
Fifth	Wood
Sixth	Sugar candy
Seventh	Wool or copper
Eighth	Pottery or bronze
Ninth	Pottery or willow
Tenth	Tin or aluminium jewellery

ONE YEAR ON

The first year of marriage is traditionally commemorated with paper. Gifts can include books, theatre tickets and art prints. In the featured display (below left), incorporating a stationery set in a wicker holder, a papier mâché box and cut-out card, the paper theme is emphasized by the inclusion of paper ribbon. It can be bought from the florist to the length you require. Untwist the tightly furled ribbon carefully and open it out slowly along its length. When untwisted, the ribbon resembles faded fabric and part of its appeal depends on its natural creases.

Flowers and foliage repeat the simplicity of the gifts. Late flowering loosestrife (*Lysimachia punctata*) and daisy-like feverfew (*Chrysanthemum parthenium*) are combined with figwort (*Scrophularia*) and delicate lady's mantle (*Alchemilla mollis*).

FIVE YEARS ON

A gift in wood traditionally commemorates the fifth wedding anniversary. You could select a gift to supplement an existing collection or begin a new one.

Combine articles made from different wood types to maximise colour and texture. The gleam of the glossy elm candlestick and goblet in the featured design (below right), is emphasized by an unpolished sycamore platter and golden miniature clogs. Dried pine cones, which can be collected in the late summer, and lotus pods from a florist, extend the woody image. If a waterproof liner is inserted, the goblet will hold flowers but filling it with water will damage it. Two plastic dishes of florist's foam on each side of the candlestick hold matching foliage arrangements. Yellow-edged hosta leaves, golden privet, common sorrel and ferns are complemented by the purplish-red *Berberis thunbergii* 'Rose Glow'.

CHRISTENINGS

Flowers are an essential part of the christening ceremony. Use them to adorn the church and help to set the scene at the reception for a memorable family occasion.

Christenings are among the most joyous and the most formal of events and they provide the perfect opportunity for family and friends to wear corsage and button-hole flowers. Another attractive idea is to fix a spray of fresh flowers to a clutch purse or to make a tiny fresh or dried-flower posy to decorate a special book mark for the parent's hymn book. A floral arrangement also makes a thoughtful present for the proud new mother or grandmother. Make a gift of a basket of roses and gypsophila or a dried-flower display to keep as a lasting memento of a happy occasion.

The usual colours chosen for christening flowers are pale pastels, the traditional colours are pink for a girl, and blue for a boy. For those who prefer not to colour-stereotype their offspring, butter-milk yellow, cream or sparkling white is appropriate. Arrangements in more vibrant colours look too dominant.

For a simple style of arrangement in the church, place simple vases of flowers on windowsills close to the font. A white or cream jug filled with lilies and gypsophila or a shower of white or cream roses looks most effective. Arrange a glass candle-stick with a large white candle and a bowl filled with floating flowers on a nearby windowsill. Those with waxy petals, such as lilies, irises, gladioli or short sprays of choisya are most suitable.

If flowers are allowed on the font, twine a length of smilax (*Asparagus asparagoides*) around its length from top to bottom, and tuck in, or wire on, a few flowers among the leaves. Alternatively, use similar greenery to encircle the base of the font and place smaller containers of flowers at intervals around it. However, it is always important to check with the vicar or priest first, as it is the policy of some churches not to allow flowers or decorations of any kind on or around the font.

Formal floral decorations are also appropriate for a christening, as this beautiful, classic display illustrates. (LEFT)

Banks of blue-white hydrangeas behind the table, a spray of fragrant blossom on the cloth and a glass bowl of multi-petalled double paeonies towering above the party fare sets the scene for a christening tea in the garden. (BELOW)

Seasonal Displays

CHRISTMAS AND EASTER ARE MADE INTO MORE SPECIAL CELEBRATIONS WITH FLOWERS

Christmas

At Christmas time with so many seasonal decorations to catch the eye, a few fresh flowers go a long way – which is just as well, considering their cost at this time of year. Blend a few large, showy flowers with evergreens – the foliage will ensure a generous appearance; make a feature of single blooms in wine glasses – perhaps one at each place for a small party – and make a ring of flowers – spray carnations are ideal – around the top of a pair of tall candlesticks.

Use cut flower food in the water to keep the flowers fresh throughout the holiday.

If you don't have the space or the inclination for a Christmas tree, use evergreen branches as a substitute, simply hang the stems with cones, baubles, clusters of nuts, dried flowers and for the children, chocolate decorations.

If you run out of time during the Christmas period, don't worry, even last minute designs can be dazzling. Fill ordinary glass tumblers, or pile plates and saucers with tiny baubles. Tuck in a few dried flowers for effect and the tiny decorations act like mirrors. Thread and knot twine through bauble loops and hang them, like fairy lights over a mantelpiece or around a mirror frame, or let them hang in a cluster like giant sparkling berries, a great welcome in the hallway.

It's a time for a spark of imagination, a dash of inspiration, and a myriad of decorative ideas.

Easter

Traditional colour and festive accessories give the lead to Easter flower arrangements that are both seasonal and fun. Whether you take time over decorating individual eggs for use in a display, or simply place a variety of budding branches in a vase and watch them slowly open out, Easter should be a celebration of spring flowers within the home.

For a simple pretty table feature, partly fill a shallow basket or bowl with shredded paper, arrange a mound of decorated eggs, and then insert one or two phials or tubes of water, or pieces of soaked foam wrapped in foil. Add some flowers to the phials, for example, anemones, primulas or wallflowers would be ideal, and complete with long-lasting leaves such as variegated ivy.

In the same vein, and for the simplest of festive displays, arrange some chocolate or hen's eggs in a bowl and tuck a few dried flowers in between.

Eggs also look attractive as a hanging festive decoration. Stick narrow ribbon around the 'waist' of the eggs and around the other way, from top to bottom. Tie at the top, leaving enough ribbon to make a loop from which to hang the egg. You could perhaps hang them from a branch as in the picture.

Painted eggs, with their solid, rounded shape, can become a seasonal focal point, tucked in close to the centre and base of a medium-sized arrangement. Adjust the number of eggs you use according to the proportions of your arrangement and flowers.

Hand-painted eggs hanging from branches make a novel Easter decoration. The eggs are blown first, and then painted in bright spring shades. (ABOVE)

As a bright surprise for Easter Sunday breakfast or tea, decorate hard-boiled eggs with the natural shape and shade of real flowers and plants. (LEFT)

Just because a fireplace is not in use, there's no need to leave it out in the cold! These bright and colourful swags make sure that it retains its rightful place as the focal point of the room. Cones, silk leaves and brilliant red fruit look-alikes are tied to scarlet ribbons to make an original and festive design. (FAR LEFT)

73

CHRISTMAS DISPLAYS

All the best Christmas decorations require is a little imagination – here are some ideas.

Plan your decorations room by room, making a cool appraisal of any areas which could do with a festive face-lift; where there is a usable flat surface for a floor arrangement or a blank wall for an evergreen wreath; a dark corner that would benefit from a jug of white everlastings, a high ceiling that would show off a hanging decoration to advantage.

The next thing to decide is an overall colour theme. Are you going to be traditional and go for holly green, berry red, or snowy white – or a combination of all three? Are you going to make this Christmas a real sparkler, and add more touches of silver or gold to your scheme – easy to do with chain-store baubles, paintsprayed twigs, nuts and seedheads – or go even further and plan your decorations around a totally different colour theme such as zingy orange or brilliant blue?

Consider which approach would do most to flatter your home and – to be totally practical – which would be the easiest to achieve by adding to and adapting the materials you already have.

GOING FOR GREEN

Evergreens are always varied and versatile. Graduate from the traditional trick of tucking a sprig of holly behind the picture and mirror frames to working on a larger scale, outlining doors and window frames.

Time may be the deciding factor in exactly how you do this. The quickest way – which works well for lightweight stems such as ivy and mistletoe – is to press them to the surface, using sticky fixing pads to hold them in place. Outline the edge of bookshelves, in a similar way.

PERFECT SETTINGS

Walls, doors and windows make perfect

Lit by four white candles, this wreath of evergreen sprays, dried golden flowerheads and silver honesty will transform a sombre corner or decorate a Christmas dinner table. (RIGHT)

backgrounds for rings, hoops or wreaths of evergreens. Whether you choose to make a wall-hanging decoration, an Advent wreath as a table centre or a traditional kissing ring, a hoop of evergreens offers generations of tradition and visual appeal.

TRIMMING THE TREE

Dried flowers make some of the most charming Christmas tree ornaments and

can also make novel presents.

Make the flowers into tiny, ribbon-tied bunches and, perhaps, wrap them in paper doilies; fill mini baskets with flowerheads and sprigs, or with paint-sprayed nuts; make small shapes from coat-hanger wire and cover them with small dried flowers as dainty tree 'mobiles'; sandwich pretty pressed flowers – pansies are perfect – between squares of transparent plastic and hang them from the tree with ribbons. The fairy lights work wonders on translucent flowers.

TAKING TO THE FLOOR

With space at such a premium at holiday-times, and most flat surfaces filled with a multitude of tempting goodies, the floor could well be the creative designer's last resort.

As a general rule, the simpler the better is the safest guideline for floor designs – do be sure to use sturdy containers. A large jug of evergreens – with or without added ingredients – can be a decorative boon in a room corner, filling an awkward gap when the furniture has been rearranged for a large gathering.

A basket of cones highlighted by a few twinkling glass baubles; a couple of trails of ivy tucked in amongst the logs in a basket; a pot of scarlet poinsettias filling an unused fireplace; designs do not have to be complicated or time-consuming to be effective.

Hanging pomander-type decorations and a pot of Christmas roses are given a warm glow by a festive candle. (FAR LEFT)

Dried flowers make unusual and dainty tree decorations, from the top, left to right: a small dried flower posy, the stems tied with ribbon; two white curtain rings trimmed with ribbon-lace bows and dried flowers; and a miniature straw basket packed with golden and white flowers and dried santolina leaves. (LEFT)

CHRISTMAS GARLANDS

A Christmas wreath is a traditional favourite and one that you create is extra special.

Christmas wreaths and garlands are on sale from the end of November onwards but it is just as easy to make your own. It's also cheaper – for the cost of a plain ready-made wreath, you can buy what you need to make your own, including the festive decorations.

CHOOSING THE MATERIAL

Foliage is the mainstay of most Christmas wreaths and garlands and there is a long tradition of using holly, ivy and conifers at Christmas-time. Of the broad-leaved evergreens, plain-leaved ivy and variegated holly are best. There are dozens of variegated hollies, with silver or gold splashes, stripes or edges, any of which are fine. Or you might choose variegated ivy – again, there are dozens available – partnered with plain-leaved holly. Keep away from too many different variegations, though, or you'll end up with a confused effect. If you can't get variegated ivy or holly, variegated elaeagnus would be a good substitute.

Cupressus, or true cypress, and its close relative, chamaecyparis, or false cypress, and Leyland's cypress also make good foliage, and branches of these quick-growing screen and hedging plants are often included by florists in mixed bunches so they're fairly easy to buy.

Whatever foliage you choose, it helps to lay it all out in separate piles in front of you when you work. Buy generous sized bunches – you can always use what's left in other floral displays, and it's better than running out halfway through.

Holly berries are a traditional Christmas decoration, but birds tend to strip holly berries long before December 25th. You can pick some berried sprigs in advance and keep them fresh in a polythene bag in a cool place. If the berries start to shrivel, spray them lightly.

ADDING FESTIVE INGREDIENTS

Once you have formed the basis of your wreath you can let your imagination and creativity run wild when deciding on additional materials to make it both sumptuous and eye-catching for Christmas. Use traditional red and gold coloured ingredients; red and gold ribbons to make large bows, and short candles for a table-top arrangement, or tall ones for a sideboard, to add light and lustre to your design. Wire nuts and cones and spray them gold and silver, or sprinkle them with a covering of glitter so that they shimmer in the candlelight, or simply varnish them if they are to be mixed with brightly-coloured flowers.

CHOOSING THE FRAME

There are many types of frame for Christmas wreaths and garlands but we have used the simplest here – copper wire formed into a rough circle. Don't worry about a perfect shape – once you get a thick cover of foliage over the wire, any unevenness is less obvious, and the slight variation on a perfect circle gives it character. If you're really keen on a perfect circle, you could use a wire-frame lampshade base instead.

You can buy plastic-backed foam

WIRING CANDLES

Table top garlands make wonderfully festive dining table centrepieces. Add short red candles to provide bright highlights to a predominantly green base. Cut a piece of thick stub wire, approximately 15-20cm (6-8in) long, in half. Insert the two pieces, spaced evenly apart, into the base of the candle. Don't insert them too near the rim, or the wax may chip off.

rings, in a range of diameters and in oval or round shapes: our dining table wreath is built on a foam ring. A more traditional foundation is wire-mesh netting formed into a circular tube and stuffed with moss. Unfortunately, moss tends to stain white paint or wallpaper so is often unsuitable for indoors. For a rustic dried wreath, teased-out straw (available from pet shops) can be bound into a long sausage shape with natural twine, then tied together at the ends to form a circular base.

DISPLAYING YOUR WREATH

The front door is the traditional location for Christmas wreaths but they look equally as nice on internal doors. Wreaths made with dried flowers or herbs must be kept under cover, as rain or even a damp atmosphere will ruin them. Indoors, you can hang a wreath over a mantlepiece mirror, from a picture hook on a wall, or on an ornate piece of furniture.

Welcome Christmas visitors with a holly garland festooned with a bright red ribbon to decorate your front door. (ABOVE)

A flat wreath makes a perfect dining-table display. Here, a plastic, pre-formed ring is covered with fresh moss, then studded with ribbons, pine cones and candles. Real and fake holly, complete with berries, ivy, fake silver leaves and red-dyed dried moss, add colour and texture. Dried artichokes and a lotus seed pod form unusual focal points. (LEFT)

STEP *by* STEP

Christmas Table display

Part of the joy of Christmas is decorating the house, and this is when seasonal dried flower displays come into their own. You can even make them in advance, so you're free to concentrate on keeping family and friends well fed and happy in the peak period. Then, when the festivities are over, you can carefully pack the displays away or dismantle them and re-arrange them for next year.

This centrepiece obeys one of the most important rules of dining table flower arrangements: the display must be low enough for everyone to see each other across the table. Otherwise, conversation can't flow easily.

CHOOSING THE MATERIALS

Only two types of flowers are used; helichrysum and safari grass. The larger ones are yellow and orange helichrysums, or straw flowers. Red helichrysums would be a more traditional choice of colour for Christmas, but the yellow and orange echo the gold of the accessories and gilded conifer cones. The smaller flowers are bleached safari grass, also called 'broom bloom'. These add a delicate touch and, because they are neutral, will blend in with any decor. Use dried gypsophila, if you can't find safari grass.

PRESERVED FOLIAGE

Cones, seeds pods and preserved foliage make up the bulk of the display. Beech mast (the empty seedheads of the beech tree) look like open flowers with petals of pale wood. They have no stems, so are wired into natural-looking groups, as well as singly. The wire would be visible in the finished display, so it is camouflaged here with brown florist's tape. The large larch cones are also wired, while the smaller ones are used still attached to their own leafless branches.

GLYCERINING BEECH

The rich brown leaves are those of glycerined beech. Beech leaves are among the easiest and most popular to glycerine – the secret is to pick and preserve them in the summer, before they go brown naturally. The delicacy of woodland fern is captured with the pressed fronds of the male fern, *Dryopteris filix-mas*, but any fern would do equally well.

The non-floral material – candles, gold ribbon, gold spray and pre-wired baubles – is available from gift shops.

CHOOSING THE CONTAINER

The base for this display is a commercially prepared teak board, cut with a band saw and carved to give the gently sculpted effect. Your florist may be able to order one for you if you give enough notice (Christmas is the busiest time of the year for florists, so don't leave it too late). Though beautiful, teak is one of the hardest woods to work. If you want to make the base yourself, a softwood, such as deal or larch, would be a better choice. You could also stain or oil the wood, to enrich its colour.

Alternatively, use an old, oval breadboard or a thick, woven straw place mat.

WATCHPOINTS

Dried flowers are highly flammable, so before lighting the candles for this or any other dried arrangement make sure that dried material is positioned well away from the candle flames. Be careful not to let the candles burn down to a dangerously low level. Do not light candles anywhere near curtains in case they 'catch'. Don't leave your display unattended, particularly if children are around, and lastly, make sure that lighted candles are extinguished before leaving the room.

Glowing warmth and the spirit of Christmas is captured in this festive dining-table arrangement. Made with dried flowers, foliage, cones and seed pods, the display is given a distinctly seasonal touch with gold ribbons, baubles and elegant tapering candles.
(FAR RIGHT)

MAKING RIBBON BOWS

1 Take a length of ribbon about 60cm (24in) long and beginning at one end, leaving a small tail, loop the ribbon into a figure of eight. Hold the point where you are forming the loops firmly between thumb and forefinger.
2 Holding the centre of the figure of eight, make a second figure of eight on top of the first. Hold the ribbon securely as you work.
3 Pinch together the point you are holding and bind with stub wire to secure the bow. Cut the wire, leaving 10cm (4in) to push into the foam.

MAKING A FESTIVE TABLE DECORATION

YOU WILL NEED

1 *8 helichrysum flowerheads in gold and orange (or in colours of your choice)*
2 *10-12 safari grass stems*
3 *6 large larch cones and 2 branches with cones on*
4 *2 sprays of beech mast*
5 *12 beech leaves*
6 *7-8 single stems of fern*
7 *2 slim cream candles*
8 *2 ribbons*
9 *5 baubles*
10 *wooden base*
11 *block of dry florist's foam*
12 *plastic flower-pot saucer*
13 *tape*
14 *wire*
15 *florist's scissors*
   gold spray paint

1

2

3

4

5

6

1 Cut a foam block to fit in a plastic flower-pot saucer Tape the block in place, then spray everything gold. When dry, position it slightly off-centre on the base, then fix it firmly. Slightly shorten one candle, then tape cocktail sticks to the ends of both candles to make insertion easier. Fix them in the foam.

2 Cut the beech diagonally into sprigs. Use seven sprigs, evenly spaced, to set the width. Place long sprigs of safari grass over the longest length of base and shorter pieces all the way round, roughly parallel to the beech. Place sprigs of safari grass between the candles.

3 Trim the fern fronds, insert horizontally into the foam block, above the beech leaves. Spray the larch branches and cones gold. When dry, insert branches low down, with the longest on the right-hand side to emphasise the asymmetric design.

4 Wire up the larger sprayed gold larch cones on short stems and insert. Place some in the centre, others at the base of the candles, and the remainder on the left-hand side to balance the branches on the right.

5 Wire and tape the beech mast, singly and in 'sprigs' of two or more. Place longer sprigs on the right-hand side. Insert a cluster of three on the left-hand side. Make two ribbon loop 'flowers'. Insert one ribbon flower at the front of the display, the other at the back.

6 Place two baubles on the left-hand side of the display, and three on the right. Wire the helichrysum, fixing the smaller flowers on the long wires, and the larger flowers on shorter wires, to keep the colour close to the centre. Form a line diagonally across the display.

STEP *by* STEP

Two Christmas Decorations

 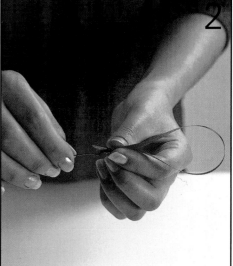

For something a little different to decorate your Christmas tree, try this unusual bauble. (BELOW)

1 Make a ribbon loop wide enough to hang over a branch of the tree. Bind the ribbon ends together with ordinary wire, leaving a long 'tail' of wire; insert the wire tail into the centre of the foam ball. Begin covering the foam ball from the base of the ribbon: attach stub wire to each of the ingredients – the berries, nuts, flowers and holly – and insert them in the foam ball in turn, so that you build up a variety of colours and textures.

2 To make tiny bows for eye-catching areas of colour, split the ribbon into thin strips. Hold the ribbon at a single point, loop it three times and then bind it with reel wire. Leave a ribbon 'tail' on each bow and twist stub wire around the tail. Insert the bows by their stub wires randomly in the foam ball.

1 Using a piece of strong wire etch a spiral guideline for the flowers from the top of the cone to the bottom. Make sure you keep the spacing even. Cover the cake board with purple felt material; glue it to the underside of the board or secure it with pins, then glue the cone to this base. Start by inserting the xeranthemums, following the etched line.

2 Next insert the silver cones, following the first line of purple flowers and then make a third line with the helichrysums (the line of cones will stand out between the flowers and give the arrangement textural contrast). Try to insert all the flowers so that their heads are pointing slightly downwards. The cone should look fairly dense and evenly-covered.

3 Break off florets from a sprayed-silver hydrangea head, wire the floret stems and insert them randomly to fill out any gaps. Make silver ribbon loops and twist stub wire around a section of each loop leaving a long enough length of wire to insert in the cone. Place the ribbon loops all over the arrangement. Lastly, insert helichrysum flowers in the top of the cone.

This pretty little table decoration is ideal for festive occasions. It's cheerful, glittery and easy to move from table to table too. (BELOW)

*E*ASTER DISPLAYS

Take Easter as your inspiration and decorate your home with festive spring flowers.

*T*he criss-crossing *gypsophila stems hold the daffodils and freesias in place to create an elegant floral display which is perfect for a festive Easter table setting. (BELOW)*

The easiest way of adding an Easter touch to your floral displays is to opt for a traditional colour scheme. The Easter colours are purple, blue, yellow and white and these are also the shades of some of the prettiest bulb, hothouse and wild flowers available at Easter-time so if you use the traditional colour theme, there is plenty to choose from.

Purple is the colour associated with Lent, the period immediately before Easter. The altar drapes and vestments worn in Church are purple until Easter Sunday, when they are replaced by gold or yellow and white. Purple orchis is sometimes known as 'Gethsemane' because its spotted leaves were said to be stained with Christ's blood. Seasonal purple-coloured flowers include violets, hyacinths, irises, lilac, and crocuses.

YELLOW FOR SPRING

In addition to its religious connotations, yellow is the predominant colour of spring flowers and is represented by tulips, lilies, irises, daffodils and narcissi and also branches of forsythia and mimosa.

Blue also has religious significance as it is the colour associated with the Virgin Mary and in legend the pretty blue speedwell grew on the side of the road to Calvary. Use anemones, freesias, hyacinths, grape hyacinths, irises, lilac and crocuses in your arrangements for their delightful shades of blue.

Pure white and cream flowers have an ethereal quality and a special serenity when used on their own, and, of course, are perfect mixers in a varied arrangement. The list of white or cream flowers is broadly similar to that for yellow.

FESTIVE EGGS

Eggs and their shells are the perfect accessory for an Easter arrangement as eggs have a traditional association with this holiday. A charming way to use empty egg shells is to turn them into a tiny vase for delicate flowers.

Break each egg close to the top, as you would a boiled egg, and neaten the edges to give a smooth look. Wash the egg shells thoroughly and check that the eggs are watertight and have not been accidentally cracked. Fill the shells about half full with water and stand them in the prettiest egg cups or napkin rings you can find brimming with a collection of primroses, snowdrops, primulas or violets.

Whole egg shells can be decorated to make a festive accompaniment for an Easter flower arrangement, and a unique, colourful design can be achieved easily using cans of spray paint and small tins of matt or gloss paint.

EASTER BASKETS

Baskets of all kinds are traditional Easter flower containers. If you have a basket with a tall handle, integrate this into your design by twisting long trails of ivy around it, and taping or wiring the stems at intervals to secure them. For an even prettier effect, wrap a small block of soaked foam in foil and bind it with wire or tape to one side, just off-centre of the handle. Cut short the stems of a few flowers, for example anemones or narcissi, and insert them into the foam. Arrange the flowers so that some are pressed in very close to the foam to conceal it and others follow the line of the handle around on each side.

Choose the blooms you use in the arrangement in order to carry the theme of the handle down to the main body of flowers. You could, for example, cover the handle of a basket with anemones. Then fill the basket itself with fragrant stems of mauve and white lilac, and thick clusters of ornamental fruit blossom, into which you have inserted a few matching anemones.

Eggs are an essential part of the Easter tradition, here they combine with fresh spring flowers to create a rustic ensemble. (ABOVE)

STEP *by* STEP
Floral Egg Nest

An Easter nest decorated with dried flowers is an inventive and seasonal way of presenting chocolate or hard-boiled eggs. You can make this basket weeks in advance of Easter to avoid extra work in the holiday period, and add the eggs just before you want to display it.

The colour theme of the display featured in the step-by-step is pastel-pink, blue and white, with touches of gold and the natural browns of the twiggy basket. This display can be adapted for an all-white colour scheme, but the spring appearance is liable to be lost. An all-white nest would be ideal, however, as a neutral setting for foil-wrapped chocolate Easter eggs, or brightly dyed, hard-boiled hen or duck eggs. A white-painted basket containing white eggs and decorated with all-white flowers would be exactly right for an Easter decoration in a more modern interior.

CHOOSING THE BASKET

The basket used for this display is handmade. Dried ferns and leaves have been interwoven among the twigs and pale raffia binding round the top adds a decorative touch. Its rough thickness and nest-like appearance makes this basket an ideal setting for eggs. Your florist should have such a basket in stock, or will be able to order one. The basket featured is 25cm (10in) in diameter, but the design is easy to scale down or up.

Any thinner, woven willow wicker baskets, such as the old-fashioned ones used to collect free-range eggs, would also be suitable. Although the basket featured is handleless, you could use a basket with a handle and make a feature of it by tying a toning ribbon bow on the top or side. If you do use a handled basket, choose one that is substantial. Natural-toned wickerwork material is nest-like in appearance,

Create the perfect Easter arrangement with a dried-flower basket filled with chocolate eggs, wooden eggs or the genuine article. (FAR RIGHT)

DRYING AND FIXING MOSS

● Moss can be bought from florists, but it is easy to collect and dry your own. To dry, lie a single layer of moss in a box lined with crumpled newspaper. Do not pack the moss tightly, as this will cause it to rot. Leave the box in a warm, dry place and in a few days the moss will have dried out.
● In order to fix the dried moss to a base, trim the lower portions of each clump, using scissors to an even thickness of about 2.5cm (1in). Cut medium-gauge stub wires into 8cm (3½in) lengths, long enough for the wires, when bent in half, to reach through the moss into the foam block. Bend each one in half, then insert, prongs facing downwards.

but, if you prefer, you could use a painted basket to tone with one of the pastel colours of the flowers, or the colour scheme of the room in which it is to be displayed.

This is an ideal display for a stripped-pine kitchen dresser, or for the centre-piece of a country-kitchen table. It is also low enough to make a table display at Easter Sunday lunch.

AFTER EASTER

Once Easter is over, you can carefully wrap the nest in lots of tissue paper and store it in a cardboard box in a well ventilated, dry spot until next year. Alternatively, you may wish to keep the basket on display for longer. To give the basket a new lease of life, remove the foam block and reindeer moss, and fill the basket with seasonal pot plants, such as small primulas. Or, if you prefer, you could use this versatile basket as a novel and rustic container for some sweet-smelling pot pourri. Another possibility is to make a dried-flower display within the basket, or even to fill it with fresh flowers, their stems concealed in a shallow jar of water.

CREATING A DRIED-FLOWER EASTER DISPLAY

YOU WILL NEED

1 *bunch of yellow flax*
2 *large bunch of sea lavender*
3 *bunch of pink helichrysum*
4 *bunch of blue larkspur*
5 *20 pieces (one bag) of reindeer moss*
6 *half a dozen hard-boiled eggs*
7 *basket*
8 *stub wire*
9 *block of dry florist's foam*
10 *scissors*

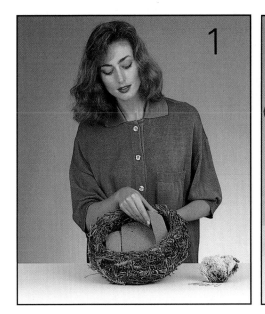

1 Cut a block of foam to fill the basket. Roughly round the corners of the short ends, following the curve of the basket. Slice the block crossways so that when inserted in the basket it finishes 5cm (2in) below the rim. Cut two side panels to the same thickness and wedge either side of the main block.

2 Completely cover the foam block with reindeer moss. Lay the clumps of moss on their sides and slice through the lower brown portion. To hold the moss in position, make wire pins out of stub wires (see box). Pin moss round the edge of the basket, working in towards the middle.

3 Cut 10-12 helichrysum stems, 8cm (3½in) long. Cut the larkspur and statice into sprigs of the same length. Make a small spray of the flowers. Bind with stub wire, then push the wire through the outside of the basket. Pull it round the rim to form a loop and thread back into the basket to secure.

4 Make up and bind another spray of dried flowers, as before, with statice behind a cluster of yellow flax. Attach the spray to the basket so that it overlaps the cut stems of the first bunch and conceals the wires. Work round the rim.

5 Continue wiring up the florets in different combinations. Attach to the rim of the basket, until it is completely covered. When you reach the end, carefully secure the stems of the last flowers under the heads of the first floret to hide the fixing wire.

6 Make any adjustments needed; when you are satisfied that the rim of flowers is evenly dense and the colour is well distributed, add the eggs. Hard-boil any hen's eggs to be displayed in the basket.

STEP *by* STEP

Easter Tree

Give your children or grandchildren a special Easter this year, with this unusual Easter tree. It's easy and inexpensive to make, and large enough to create an impact in any room. By omitting the ducks and fluffy chicks, you can give the tree more sophisticated overtones, perhaps for an Easter dinner party.

Most of the ingredients used give double value for money: the flower pot container can go in the garden aferwards, the sweet decorations can be eaten, and the Easter trinkets put away for use next year.

CHOOSING THE FLOWERS
Traditional Easter colours, yellow and white are used here, but you could use pastel colours, in a monochromatic or multi-coloured room scheme.

You will need a bunch of large yellow daffodils. Our featured blooms have orange-tinged trumpets, but yellow, yellow and white, creamy-white trumpets or the scented, small-flowered 'Paperwhite' or 'Soleil d'Or' could be used. Buy a bunch with leaves as well as flowers, to re-create the look of a clump of daffodils growing in the wild.

The small-flowered narcissus should be just starting to open. When you get the flowers home, snip off the lower, white stems to the required display length and soak them separately from other flowers, as daffodil stems exude a slimy sap that can block the stems of other flowers and shorten their lives.

Use a bunch of white tulips or bright yellow ones, especially if you're using white daffodils. Instead of ordinary, single tulips, you could buy the more expensive double-flowered blooms, such as the yellow 'Monte Carlo'. Buy tulips closed, but with the buds showing colour. Again, condition them in a tall container with water halfway up their stems, ideally overnight. Buy mimosa, the most ex-

pensive ingredient, with about half the buds open. Re-cut the stems and give them a long drink of water. A budget alternative is forsythia, from the florist or the garden. Combine it with ferns or other dark-green, delicate foliage.

Shasta daisies from a florist add to the informal touch. Choose full-open flowers with hard centres; fluffy centres indicate an over-mature flower.

CHOOSING THE TREE AND MOSS
Hazel, with its elegant branches and delicate catkins, makes an ideal choice. The catkins will continue to grow, even when the branches are cut. A few green leaves may appear, as the warm conditions in your home force the branches into new spring growth.

Alternatives include alder, beech, birch or even lilac. Oak branches would give the effect of a stubby tree, like a miniature oak, while Peking, or contorted, willow has a sophisticated, oriental-style appeal.

Try to choose attractively forked branches as straight ones provide no hooks for the decorations, and they would simply slide to the base. Avoid conifer branches, as they have Christmas overtones, even in spring. Conceal the top of the foam block with bun moss, and continue the wild garden theme. You can order bun moss from your florist.

CHOOSING A CONTAINER
An ordinary, terracotta flower pot, 15cm (6in) across, is used here. Inexpensive and heavy enough to balance the top-heavy weight of the tree, a flower pot adds to the informal, garden appearance. For a more sophisticated look, spray a flower pot, with one or more colours, to tone in with the yellow and white theme, or the colour scheme of the room.

Alternatively, you could use a glazed

Celebrate Easter in style, with this unusual Easter tree. Made of hazel branches adorned with foil-covered treats and festive decorations and inserted into a foam-filled flower pot, the tree has its own colourful garden of tulips, mimosa, daffodils and shasta daisies, nestling in a bed of bun moss. (FAR RIGHT)

ceramic storage jar or simple vase, in a suitable colour, or a cylindrical glass storage jar or bowl lined with moss, to conceal the foam block. Plastic flower pots aren't really suitable, as they are lightweight and liable to topple over. When you put a lot of time and effort into creating a display, you should always try to show it off to its best advantage.

tiny, fluffy, chicks to the branches – they often have flexible wire feet which can be bent into any shape. Or buy narrow ribbon, in white, pale and deep yellow, and tie little bows on the branches. If you intend to eat the unwrapped marzipan and chocolates, don't hang them too far in advance, otherwise they may get dry and dusty.

CHOOSING DECORATIONS

Here, foil-covered chocolate coins and eggs, unwrapped chocolates, marzipan fruit and tiny wicker baskets are hung from the branches.

You could fix foil-covered sweets or

CHOOSING A SETTING

The Easter tree, like a Christmas tree, should be given pride of place, with plenty of space around it to allow people to walk by without damaging it. If it is safe from young children and pets, you could

PREPARING A FESTIVE EASTER TREE

YOU WILL NEED

1 *1 hazel branch with catkins*
2 *8 yellow and orange daffodils*
3 *5 white tulips*
4 *1 large bunch of mimosa*
5 *10 white shasta daisies*
6 *1 large clump of bun moss*
7 *assorted hanging chocolates and novelties*
8 *floristry scissors*
9 *block of wet florist's foam*
10 *15cm (6in) stub wires*
11 *terracotta pot*
12 *polythene film*

1

2

3

4

5

6

1 Prepare your terracotta pot as shown in the box. Place the hazel branch with catkins into the centre of the pot and push it firmly into the foam. The branch should stand around 75cm (30in) high and have plenty of forked twigs on which to hang the festive decorations.

2 Insert the ready-cut daffodils of various lengths. Make sure that the stems are not too long, otherwise you won't be able to see the decorations. Arrange the daffodils in the foam, clustered vertically around the base of the branch. Tie a few loose leaves together with wire and push them into the foam.

3 Trim the tulips to different lengths and remove most of the leaves. Wrap some of the leaves around your finger to make them curl and push them in between the daffodil stems. Arrange the tulip blooms and the remaining leaves evenly around the outside of the display.

4 Cut most of the leaves off one large stem of mimosa and snip off the sideshoots so you have a cluster of smaller sprigs. Insert both flowers and foliage around the rim of the pot to make a collar. Place a few stems upright and angle others outward.

5 Trim the lower leaves off the shasta daisies and scatter them in a circle throughout the other flowers. Remember to keep the other stems fairly short so the lower twigs of the hazel branch are still visible.

6 Finally, hang the Easter novelties. Place the lighter decorations on the higher and more flimsy branches. Then hang the heavier novelties onto the larger, stronger branches. Arrange the fluffy chicks among the flowers to complete the display.

use it as a floor-level display, otherwise place it on a low table or chair.

Place the tree in a cool position as mimosa doesn't like heat. Mimosa is also vulnerable to ethylene gas, so keep it well away from fruit, vegetables and wilted flowers.

LOOKING AFTER THE DISPLAY

If children want to remove the trinkets and sweets, a bit of gentle guidance will keep them from knocking the display over in their enthusiasm.

Even after the decorations are re-moved, the tree on its flowery knoll remains an attractive display of colour.

Remember to top up the water, and mist-spray the moss regularly, to keep it fresh and green. Daffodils are short-lived; once the flowers turn papery, carefully remove them and replace with fresh buds. Gather any mimosa flowers that fall from the branches, and discard or save them for pot pourri. When you dismantle the

display, save the hazel branches to sup-port sweet peas or herbaceous perennials, such as delphiniums, in the summer garden.

MARZIPAN FRUIT

Marzipan fruit is expensive to buy but easy to make and can be tinted with food dye to the desired colour. Handle marzipan lightly at room temperature, as it gets oily if over-worked. Form grape-sized pieces into fruit shapes such as apples and pears. Stick in cloves as stalks and paint detail on the fruit with a fine brush and diluted food colouring. Roll the fruit in caster sugar for a crystalline surface. With a large needle, pierce a hole through the top, a quarter of the way down. Place in a dry, cool, airy spot for one or two days to harden. Hang from gold thread.

PREPARING THE TERRACOTTA POT

1 Line a clean pot with polythene or a plastic bag to prevent water from leaking out of the porous terracotta. Fit in the trimmed and soaked florist's foam. Ensure that none of the foam shows over the pot edge.
2 Trim the edges of the plastic back to the level of the pot rim.

Add a little more water into the pot to ensure the foam is wet enough.
3 Cover the top of the foam with small clumps of bun moss to create a natural woodland effect. Fix in position with hairpin-shaped stub wires. Leave gaps to insert the flower steps.

EASTER TABLES

Make sure your table is prepared for the Easter holiday by planning one or two unusual flower arrangements.

When flower-arranging at Easter, try to compose a couple of designs which are completely different in appearance; one a casual grouping of bright and cheerful spring flowers to reflect the festive atmosphere at Easter, and another more elegant arrangement to signify the serious religious aspect of the celebrations.

Flowers for the breakfast table should not look contrived, so a jug of spring blooms carefully chosen to complement one key colour in the room is really all that is needed. In order to make a bunch of spring flowers look most effective, you will need a deep, wide-necked container such as a jug or storage jar. Choose a combination of irises, tulips, daffodils, anemones, hyacinths, broom or periwinkle and ensure that the stems are of varying lengths. Start using tall buds and flowers for the centre. Hold them in one hand and place slightly shorter stems around them. Continue in this fashion until you have included the shortest stems. Once you have achieved a pleasing look, place in water.

Select your most stylish container for the formal Easter arrangement. A basket with a low handle will look attractive with flowers in a graceful curve, and a shallow bowl lends itself to flowers arranged in a gentle mound.

Foam-filled rings are available from florist shops and can be transformed into a fresh-flower hoop for the table centre. For an Easter display with religious overtones, create a dramatic ring with twigs to represent the crown of thorns.

Blue, purple and yellow flowers, in the traditional Easter shades, are arranged in pale brown pots which look like loaves. (BELOW)

A graceful swan and cygnet vase is the vessel for this elegant arrangement of pink broom, red and white tulips and narcissi. (LEFT)

Index